The Best Slow Cooker Cookbook Ever

Natalie Haughton

A John Boswell Associates/King Hill Productions Book
HarperCollins*Publishers*

HarperCollins books may be purchased for educational, business, or sales promotional use. For information, please write: Special Markets Department, HarperCollins Publishers, Inc., 10 East 53rd Street, New York, NY 10022.

FIRST EDITION

Design: Barbara Cohen Aronica
Index: Maro Riofrancos

Library of Congress Cataloging-in-Publication Data

Haughton, Natalie Hartanov.
    The best slow cooker bookbook ever / Natalie Haughton. — 1st ed.
      p.   cm.
    "A John Boswell Associates/King Hill Productions book."
    Includes index.
    ISBN 0-06-017266-5
    1. Electric cookery. Slow.   I. Title.
TX827.H38   1995
   641.5'884—dc20   95-37509

00 01 02 HC 20 19 18 17 16 15 14 13 12

Acknowledgments

Special thanks to the slow cooker manufacturers who provided equipment to use in recipe testing: The Rival Company, Hamilton Beach/Proctor-Silex, Inc., National Presto Industries, Inc., Dazey Corporation, and The West Bend Company. Gratitude to Dr. George K. York, Extension Food Microbiologist Emeritus, Department of Food Science and Technology, University of California, Davis, California, for his invaluable food expertise and help, to Patti Gray for her special talents in helping with recipe inspirations and development, and to Susan Wyler, my editor, for continued support and making this book a reality. Thanks, too, to Fred, Alexis, Grant, Mom and Dad, and all of the other taste testers, who generously shared their palates and opinions.

Contents

Introduction

Slow and Steady Wins the Race

Ever since it made its way into the American kitchen in the early 1970s, millions of cooks throughout the country have been using the electric slow cooker, or crockery pot, best known by the popular Rival trademarked name: Crock-Pot. And for good reason. Slow cookers are convenient and simple to use; they are cost- and time-efficient and require no watching or tending. Once everything is in the pot, you can walk away for several hours, or overnight, and return to a completed dish. Dips, soups, stews, casseroles, vegetables, beans, preserves, desserts, and hot drinks all attest to the slow cooker's versatility.

Slow cookers enable busy people to put dinner on the table effortlessly and often economically, as many of the creations suited to the pot utilize less expensive, less tender cuts of meat as well as beans, potatoes, and other foods that are good buys and ideal for long, slow simmering. Most slow-cooker recipes rely on items readily available in supermarkets and don't require long lists of exotic ingredients. Other than chopping or the quick mixing of ingredients, it's simply a matter of tossing everything into the pot. With a very few exceptions—ground beef or ground turkey is browned first, for instance—no other cooking is needed. It's not even necessary to precook or presoak dried beans!

There are other reasons to opt for a slow cooker as well. Heating up the kitchen is avoided. In most recipes, no stirring is required during cooking. Scorching is eliminated and shrinkage of meats is reduced due to the long, low heat. Slow cookers are energy efficient. And they are an asset to party and potluck cooks who want to keep foods warm and serve them right from the pot.

Since they are designed for slow, moist-heat cooking, food technologists now agree that slow cookers are perfectly safe. Even at the low-heat temperature setting, slow cookers raise the internal temperature of the food well beyond 140 degrees F, the minimum temperature at which bacteria are killed. (Bacterial growth is inhibited at temperatures above 130 degrees F.) On low heat, meats and poultry will easily reach the recommended temperatures suggested by food safety experts and often will go much higher, depending on the length of the cooking time: beef, 150 to 165 degrees F; pork, 165 to 175 degrees F (no longer pink); poultry 170 to 180 degrees F, or until the juices run clear and the meat is no longer pink or red. You can check finished dishes with a meat thermometer to be sure, but it really isn't necessary.

As foods in a slow cooker get hot, the steam produced rises, condenses into moisture on the lid, and then returns to the food in the pot. Even if it seems like too little liquid, use only the amount specified in a recipe. You'll be amazed at how much moisture will accumulate in a slow cooker from meats, poultry, and vegetables and through condensation.

Recipes in this collection run the gamut of dishes that cook at different heat settings, in different size pots, and for different lengths of time. Contrary to popular belief, not all foods should be stashed in a slow cooker and cooked for 8 to 10 hours, or while you drive across the country and back. As with other appliances, each dish has different cooking time requirements in a slow cooker. How long a recipe actually takes in a slow cooker depends on the type of food, the temperature of the food when you put it into the cooker, the size of the foods or the size pieces food are cut into, and how full the pot is filled.

In many recipes, the cooking time is critical. Generally chicken breasts cook in 3½ to 4½ hours. Appetizers and rice dishes may take even less time. And desserts, on the high heat setting, may require only 2 to 3 hours. Beverages are hot and ready to serve in 4 to 5 hours. And chili and stew cooking times vary, depending on the ingredients included. So do take note and plan accordingly.

Some of the shorter-cooking recipes can be made the night before you plan to serve them. After cooling for no longer than 2 hours, whisk them into the refrigerator. Just prior to serving, give them a quick zap in the microwave oven, and you'll have dinner on the table in short order.

If you're in a hurry, you might want to start a longer-cooking dish, such as a chili, on the high setting for the first hour of cooking time to get it going quickly and then reduce the heat setting to low as called for in the recipe.

Like other kitchen appliances, the slow cooker is not well suited to cooking all foods. Don't rely on it for cooking large tender roasts (like prime rib, standing rib, leg of lamb), tender steaks, chicken or turkey pieces with the skin on, pies, cakes, cookies, and most seafood dishes. Recipes with large amounts of natural cheese or other dairy products are also poor candidates for the slow cooker.

Slow Cooker Makes and Models

Millions of slow cookers have been sold in the United States over the last two decades. Today, there are three basic types of slow cookers available. Generally, they are categorized by the design of the heating element or the pot in general. Makes and models vary, and not all are readily available throughout the country.

The most common and best-selling type is the original slow cooker, marketed today by the granddaddy of the slow-cooker manufacturers, The Rival Company, whose name Crock-Pot is a registered trademark of the company and not a generic term, as some believe. Round in shape, it is designed simply to slow cook, which it does exceedingly well. It has a crockery insert (which may or may not be removable) and two temperature settings: low (about 200 degrees F) and high (about 300 degrees F). The heating coils are encased in the sides of the metal unit that houses the crockery insert, which allows for continuous even heat to surround the food, thus avoiding scorching and burning. On models with a removable stoneware insert, the insert is ovenproof and microwave safe, but should not be used on a gas or electric burner or under the broiler.

The metal units of this style slow cooker should not be immersed in water; however, the lids and removable liners or inserts can be. The 3½- and 5-quart sizes are Rival's biggest sellers.

Because it is the most versatile and convenient to use, has the most even and continuous heating, and is tailored to all-around cooking from appetizers to desserts, I prefer this surround-heating style of slow cooker to all of the others. The recipes in this book worked best in this type of slow cooker, which is manufactured by both Rival and Hamilton Beach/Proctor-Silex, Inc.

In addition to the two heat settings, the Hamilton Beach/Proctor-Silex models come with an Automatic Temperature Shift feature, which can cook the food on the high heat setting for 30 to 120 minutes in the beginning of the cooking time (if you opt to use the feature) and then automatically shift to low. But the cook has no way of knowing when the heat shifts to the low setting because the dial doesn't move.

Another type of slow cooker is really many appliances in one: a multipurpose cooker that steams, fries, and roasts in addition to slow cooking. Dazey Corporation and National Presto Industries, Inc., make and market this type of product, which is called respectively, Dazey Chef's Pot Plus or Stocker Plus, or Presto Kitchen Kettle Plus Crockery.

All three models come with glass lids, crockery liners for slow cooking, detachable adjustable temperature controls (which allow cooks to dial a specific cooking temperature up to 400 degrees F), and outer nonstick water-immersible metal pots. The heating element, or coil, located on the bottom of the metal pot, continuously cycles on and off during slow cooking. Be sure to refer to the manufacturer's instruction book for low and high heat setting recommendations for slow-cooking, as they vary from 250 to 350 degrees F (one manufacturer advises not using a temperature setting lower than 275 degrees F for slow cooking).

Because the heating element is at the bottom of the pot and cycles on and off during cooking, be cautious when using the recipes in this book in this type of cooker. You may need to adjust cooking times and temperatures and stir the contents of the pot every so often during cooking to avoid sticking and scorching. My dessert and appetizer recipes were unsatisfactory in this type of cooker.

The other style of slow cooker, manufactured by The West Bend Company, has a thin rectangular or round removable metal cooking vessel (with a glass or plastic cover) with a nonstick finish that sits on an electric heating base. The cooker has five heat settings, but only the three highest (low, medium, and high heat settings) should be used for cooking raw foods. The two lowest settings are only for warming (muffins or dinner rolls) or keeping cooked foods warm for serving. Prebrowning of any meats or foods can be done in the metal cooking vessel on top of the stove before placing it on the heating base and adding the other recipe ingredients.

Because the heat comes from underneath the metal pan and cycles on and off during cooking, some foods have a tendency to stick and cook unevenly in this type of cooker. Not all of the recipes in this book are well suited to cooking in this type of cooker, and some may not work at all, especially the appetizers, poultry dishes, side dishes (especially rice), and desserts. Other recipes may require stirring several times during cooking to avoid scorching. Cooks using this type of cooker should refer to their instruction manuals for recipe information.

Which Size Fits Best

Electric slow cookers come in a range of sizes, ranging from 2½ to 6 quarts. A 1-quart mini slow cooker, manufactured by Rival and known as a Crock-Ette, is also available. It lacks a switch; to turn it on, you simply plug it in. It cooks only small quantities of food and is best suited to tasks like heating party appetizers or dips or melting ingredients for a chocolate dessert fondue.

The 3½-, 4-, and 5-quart models (with removable liners) are the most popular sizes. Purchase a size suitable for your lifestyle and personal dining needs. If you plan to purchase only one pot, I'd recommend a 3½- or 4-quart model. If you'd like to make the desserts in this book that use an 8-inch springform pan or a 2½-quart soufflé dish, you'll need a 5-quart Rival Crock-Pot. You may find the slow cooker so versatile and convenient that you'll enjoy having a couple of different sizes handy to whip up several dishes at the same time.

For convenience and flexibility in both serving and cleaning up, I recommend you select a slow-cooker model with a removable ceramic or stoneware liner. Most of the removable inserts can also go into the microwave or regular oven and even into the dishwasher.

Helpful Hints

- To avoid breakage or cracking, never add cold water to a hot crockery insert. If you want to soak the hot pot immediately after the cooked food has been removed, add hot water to the hot insert.

- For best results, most manufacturers recommend that the slow cooker be half to three-quarters full. Refer to the manufacturer's instruction book accompanying your pot.

- Keep perishable foods, such as meats, poultry, fish, and vegetables, refrigerated until preparation and cooking time. If you opt to cut up vegetables or meats the night before you're planning to cook them, be sure to package each different item separately and store in the refrigerator.

- Purchase roasts and other large cuts of meats in a size and shape that will fit conveniently into your slow cooker. Otherwise, plan on trimming the meat to fit.

- To end up with the least amount of fat in finished slow-cooker dishes, use lean meats and skinless poultry, well trimmed of fat.

- In general, avoid using completely frozen foods in the slow cooker. If necessary, thaw frozen ingredients in a microwave oven before adding to the cooker.

- To avoid heat loss, refrain from removing the lid during the first three-quarters of the cooking time. If you peek often, an extension of the cooking time may be required. Remove the lid only to stir food or check for doneness.

- Use cooking times as guidelines. Pots vary; each one is not exactly the same, and fluctuations in power or voltage may occur. Generally, figure that 1 hour on high is about 2 hours on low. Some recipes should only be cooked on high or low, so follow directions carefully.

- Because they cook more slowly than meats, generally place fresh vegetables, such as carrots, potatoes, celery, and onions, in the bottom and around the sides of the slow cooker. Then place meats on top.

- For best flavor and texture, ground beef or ground turkey should usually be browned on top of the stove before adding to the slow cooker. With few exceptions, it's not necessary to brown other meats.

- To speed up the thickening of sauces with flour or cornstarch at the end of the cooking, increase the heat to the high setting and cook from 15 to 45 minutes longer. Or drain the juices into a saucepan and bring to a boil on top of the stove or in a glass measure in a microwave oven, stirring until smooth and thickened.

- To avoid curdling dairy products, generally add milk, heavy cream, sour cream, or cheeses sometime during the last hour of cooking time. If heating cheeses for long periods, opt to use processed cheeses or cheese spreads, because they can tolerate more heat. Some dessert recipes in this book use milk, cream, eggs, and cream cheese successfully, but for the most part, they are cooked quickly on the high heat setting.

- At high altitudes (more than 3,500 feet), it may be necessary to increase the cooking times specified in the recipes here.

- Flavors often become diluted with long slow cooking; so before serving any slow-cooker creation, taste and adjust the seasonings. You'll note that many of the recipes in this collection add additional spices, herbs, and other ingredients at the end of the cooking time for more pizzazz. To add spark, I also use more seasoned salt and garlic pepper than usual. If you prefer, you can substitute ordinary salt and pepper, but realize there will be a concurrent loss of taste.

- Because colors fade with long, slow cooking, for eye appeal, dress up slow-cooker dishes with a garnish of chopped fresh parsley, cilantro or watercress, basil or other fresh herbs, sliced scallions, chopped tomatoes or red peppers, shredded carrots, shredded cheeses, nonfat yogurt, sour cream, lemon or lime wedges, cooked crumbled bacon, or sliced radishes.

If you received a slow cooker as a wedding present or have one stashed on a shelf or buried in the garage, now may be a good time to dig it out and give it another chance. Explore the versatile possibilities within these pages. Of course, there are soups, stews, and chilis, but you can also use your slow cooker to turn out dried fruit chutney, mango chutney, apricot preserves, holiday drinks, and party punches, desserts including cheesecakes, and numerous other innovative dishes you probably didn't think possible.

Chapter One
Appetizers and Snacks

With an electric slow cooker, you can turn out an amazing array of enticing hot and cold appetizers and snacks, which run the gamut from casual to sophisticated, with a minimum of kitchen preparation time.

What makes the slow cooker so convenient and appealing is that, with few exceptions, no constant stirring, checking, or worrying about overcooking or burning will take its toll on the harried cook. For the most part, recipes take care of themselves in a slow cooker.

Haven't you at least once when entertaining—in the turmoil of racing around the kitchen to complete other tasks, take coats, pour drinks—forgotten to take a hot appetizer out of the oven and had it overbake or burn? With a slow cooker, it's possible to avoid such a scenario.

The Party Bean Dip is a good choice for a crowd. Once you've browned the ground beef and added it to the slow cooker, along with green olives, pinto beans, and savory seasonings, it's on its way to making itself. Cheese is stirred in just before serving. Another hot creation that's always popular is the Spinach Artichoke Dip. The base is whipped up in a food processor, then turned into a 3½-quart slow cooker. In 1½ hours it's ready to serve, topped with Jack cheese and prepared salsa and accompanied with tortilla chips or assorted cut-up vegetables for dippers.

Other dip choices include Curried Cheese Dip, Chile-Cheese Refried Bean Dip, and Chile Con Queso, which also makes a good sauce. Several of the dips rely on the 1-quart mini slow cooker, which is the ideal size for making smaller quantities and for serving smaller numbers of guests.

The slow cooker also lends itself to heating up a tasty mélange of miniature smoked sausages with an apricot preserve and mustard glaze. Serve them hot from the pot and let guests help themselves.

There's no worry about burning expensive nuts when you make Buttery Roasted Pecans and Spiced Walnuts in the slow cooker. Curried Chili Pecans and Hot Spicy Pecans provide more adventurous variations on the same theme.

The pièce de résistance in this appetizer lineup is a savory Southwestern-inspired cheesecake, baked in a springform pan in a 5-quart electric slow cooker. It's a chic conversation piece. Be sure to make it in advance and chill. Served topped with quick and easily prepared Pineapple-Tomato Salsa, it's certain to have guests clamoring for more.

Chile-Cheese Refried Bean Dip

Put this on a couple of hours before you're expecting guests for a casual gathering. Serve tortilla chips for dipping.

MAKES ABOUT 2 CUPS

1 (16-ounce) can fat-free refried beans
1 (8-ounce) package cream cheese, cut into cubes, softened
¾ cup chopped scallions
1 (4-ounce) can diced green chiles
¾ cup shredded Cheddar cheese
1 (2¼-ounce) can sliced ripe olives, rinsed and drained
Tortilla chips, for serving

1. In a 1-quart mini electric slow cooker, mix together the refried beans and cream cheese. Stir in the scallions and chiles.
2. Cover, plug in the cooker, and cook 2 hours, stirring once or twice, until very hot.
3. Mix in ½ cup cheese and the olives. Sprinkle the remaining ¼ cup cheese on top. Serve immediately with tortilla chips for dipping.

Hot Spinach Cheese Dip

Here's a slow, easy take on the favorite hot spinach dip.

1 (10-ounce) package frozen chopped spinach, thawed and drained
1 (8-ounce) package cream cheese, softened
½ cup chopped scallions
½ teaspoon garlic pepper

1 cup shredded Cheddar cheese
⅓ cup rehydrated, chopped sun-dried tomatoes or chopped drained water chestnuts
Crackers and/or cut-up assorted fresh vegetables, for serving

1. In a 1-quart mini electric slow cooker, mix together the spinach and cream cheese. Stir in the scallions and garlic pepper.
2. Cover, plug in the cooker, and cook 2 hours, stirring once or twice, until very hot.
3. Reserve 2 tablespoons cheese for the top. Stir in the remaining cheese and sun-dried tomatoes. Sprinkle the reserved cheese on top. Pass crackers and/or vegetables for dipping.

Chile Con Queso

Serve this zippy dip with tortilla chips or use as a sauce to drizzle over omelets, tomato slices on toast points, open-face hamburgers, enchiladas, burritos, grilled chicken breasts, steamed broccoli, or other vegetables.

MAKES ABOUT 2½ CUPS

1 (16-ounce) package mild Mexican pasteurized-process cheese spread with jalapeño pepper, such as Velveeta

1½ cups jarred thick and chunky salsa
Tortilla chips, for serving

1. Cut the cheese into cubes. Place in a 3½-quart electric slow cooker. Mix in the salsa.

2. Cover and cook on the low heat setting 1½ hours, stirring once or twice, until the cheese is melted and smooth.

3. Remove the lid, increase the heat to the high setting, and cook 1 to 1¼ hours longer, or until the mixture is hot throughout. Serve with tortilla chips for dipping.

Curried Cheese Dip

This curry-flavored spread is simple and irresistible.

MAKES ABOUT 1½ CUPS

2 cups shredded Cheddar cheese
1 (8-ounce) package cream cheese,
    softened
½ cup milk
¼ cup chopped scallions

1 (2¼-ounce) can sliced ripe olives,
    rinsed and drained
1½ teaspoons Madras curry powder
Cut-up assorted fresh vegetables or
    crackers, for serving

1. In a 1-quart mini electric slow cooker, mix together the cheeses, milk, scallions, olives, and curry powder.
2. Cover, plug in the cooker, and cook 45 minutes to 1 hour, or until hot. Stir to mix well. Serve with vegetables or crackers for dipping.

Party Bean Dip

This is a great choice when you're expecting a crowd. Use any leftovers to make the base of the tostada salad—pile on top of a few chips and top with shredded lettuce and cheese, chopped tomatoes, avocado, scallions, and salsa.

MAKES 4½ TO 5 CUPS

1 pound lean ground beef
1 large onion, chopped
2 (15-ounce) cans pinto beans, rinsed and drained
1 cup ketchup
1 tablespoon chili powder
1½ teaspoons ground cumin
½ teaspoon garlic powder

Pinch of cayenne, or more to taste
½ cup chopped pimiento-stuffed green olives or 1 (2¼-ounce) can sliced ripe olives, drained
1½ cups shredded Cheddar cheese
Tortilla chips and fresh cut-up vegetables, for serving

1. In a large skillet on top of the stove, cook the beef with the onion over medium-high heat, stirring, until browned, 6 to 8 minutes. Drain off any fat.

2. Turn into a 3½-quart electric slow cooker. Add the beans, mashing up to half of them with a fork. Stir in the ketchup, chili powder, cumin, garlic powder, cayenne, and olives until well mixed.

3. Cover and cook on the high heat setting 1½ hours or on the low heat setting 3 hours.

4. Stir in 1 cup of the cheese, mixing well. Top with the remaining ½ cup cheese. Serve immediately with tortilla chips and fresh vegetables. Refrigerate any leftovers.

Southwestern Appetizer Cheesecake

For a conversation piece, serve this savory, spicy appetizer topped with an easily prepared pineapple-tomato salsa at your next party. It's bound to gain raves, and guests will never believe the cheesecake was baked in a slow cooker.

MAKES 1 APPETIZER CHEESECAKE; 10 OR MORE SERVINGS

3 (8-ounce) packages cream cheese, softened
1 cup sour cream
½ cup roasted red pepper pieces
1 (1¼-ounce) package taco seasoning mix

3 eggs
2 tablespoons all-purpose flour
1 (4-ounce) can diced green chiles
Pineapple-Tomato Salsa (recipe follows)
White corn or other tortilla chips, for serving

1. In a food processor fitted with a metal blade, combine the cream cheese and sour cream; process until smooth. Add the red pepper pieces and dry taco seasoning mix and process until smooth. Add the eggs and flour and mix until smooth and thoroughly combined. By hand, stir in the green chiles.

2. Turn into an 8-inch springform pan, spreading evenly. Place the cheesecake on a vegetable steamer or other rack set in the bottom of a 5-quart electric slow cooker. Carefully add 1 cup hot water around the sides of the springform to the bottom of the slow cooker.

3. Cover with the slow cooker lid and cook on the high heat setting about 2 hours, or until set (do not attempt to cook on the low heat setting for a longer time).

4. Turn off the slow cooker. With paper towels, carefully blot any excess moisture on top of the cheesecake. Leave the lid off the slow cooker and allow the cheesecake to stand in the cooker until the pan is cool enough to handle, about 1 hour. Remove and cool the cheesecake to lukewarm; then refrigerate 3 to 4 hours or longer, until cold.

5. Just before serving, remove the springform side of the pan. Place the cheesecake on a serving platter and carefully spoon pineapple-tomato salsa on top. Serve with chips.

PINEAPPLE-TOMATO SALSA: Drain 1 (20-ounce) can unsweetened pineapple chunks well. Chop the chunks into smaller pieces. In a medium bowl, combine the pineapple pieces, 1 large tomato, chopped, 2 scallions, chopped, ½ of a small red or green bell pepper, chopped, 2 tablespoons canned diced green chiles, ¼ teaspoon garlic powder, 1 tablespoon chopped fresh cilantro or ¼ teaspoon dried basil, pinch of sugar, 1 tablespoon red wine vinegar, 2 teaspoons vegetable oil, and seasoned salt to taste. Mix well. Refrigerate until serving time to allow the flavors to blend.

Spinach Artichoke Dip

Once you've mixed up this dip in the food processor, cook it until hot throughout in a slow cooker. Serve topped with melted cheese and ringed with your favorite salsa.

2 (8-ounce) packages cream cheese, softened

¾ cup heavy cream (use half milk, if desired)

⅓ cup grated Parmesan cheese

¼ teaspoon garlic powder

1 (16-ounce) bag frozen cut leaf spinach, thawed and well drained

1 (13¾-ounce) can quartered artichoke hearts, rinsed and well drained

⅔ cup shredded Monterey Jack cheese

1 cup prepared salsa

Crackers or tortilla chips, for serving

1. In a food processor fitted with a metal blade, process the cream cheese, cream, Parmesan cheese, and garlic powder until smooth and creamy. Add the spinach and process until thoroughly mixed. Add the artichokes and process just until coarsely chopped.

2. Turn the mixture into a 3½-quart electric slow cooker; smooth the top.

3. Cover and cook on the high heat setting 1¼ to 1½ hours, until hot in the center. Sprinkle the top evenly with the Jack cheese and spoon the salsa in a ring around the inside edges of the slow cooker. Cover and continue heating on high 15 minutes longer, or until the cheese is melted. Reduce the heat to the low setting and serve warm with crackers or tortilla chips for dipping. Refrigerate any leftovers.

Glazed Cocktail Sausages

Use a mini slow cooker to heat mini smoked sausages in a mustard-apricot sauce for an easy appetizer.

MAKES 6 TO 8 SERVINGS

¾ cup apricot preserves
¼ cup prepared yellow mustard
2 scallions, chopped

½ pound precooked mini smoked
  sausages

1. In a 1-quart mini electric slow cooker, mix together the preserves and mustard. Stir in the scallions and sausages.

2. Cover, plug in the cooker, and cook 3 hours, or until very hot.

3. Remove the cover, stir to mix, and serve immediately with toothpicks; keep the heat on for another 30 to 60 minutes, if desired, while serving.

TO MAKE IN A 3½-QUART ELECTRIC SLOW COOKER: Mix together 1 (16-ounce) jar apricot preserves and ⅓ cup prepared yellow mustard. Stir in 6 chopped scallions and 2 pounds precooked mini smoked sausages. Cover and cook on the low heat setting 4½ to 5 hours, or until the sausages are hot. Makes 24 or more servings.

Buttery Roasted Pecans

Make one type of nut or several different variations to give for hostess gifts or serve at parties.

1 stick (4 ounces) butter, cut into pieces
1½ pounds (6 cups) pecan halves

1 teaspoon coarse (kosher) salt
¼ teaspoon freshly ground pepper

1. In a 3½- or 4-quart electric slow cooker, place the cut-up butter. Heat, uncovered, on the high heat setting 15 to 20 minutes, until the butter is melted. Add the pecans and stir to coat them with the butter.

2. Cover and cook on the high heat setting ½ hour. Uncover and cook on high 2½ hours longer, stirring occasionally.

3. Season the nuts with the salt and pepper. Spread the pecans on a foil-lined baking sheet to cool. Store in an airtight container in the refrigerator up to 6 weeks or freeze up to 3 months. Return to room temperature before serving or heat and serve warm.

VARIATIONS:

CURRIED CHILI PECANS: Substitute 2 teaspoons Madras curry powder and 1 teaspoon chili powder for the coarse salt.

HOT SPICY PECANS: Substitute 2 teaspoons chili powder, ½ teaspoon onion salt, and ½ teaspoon garlic powder for the coarse salt.

Spiced Walnuts

Instead of toasting flavored walnuts in the oven, use a slow cooker to do the job. Not much tending is required, and there's no chance of burning them if you follow the cooking time below.

MAKES 4 CUPS

1 pound (4 cups) walnut halves or
   large pieces
2 tablespoons olive oil
2½ teaspoons chili powder

2 tablespoons Worcestershire sauce
½ teaspoon onion powder
¼ teaspoon freshly ground pepper
¼ to ½ teaspoon coarse (kosher) salt

1. In a 3½- or 4-quart electric slow cooker, combine all the ingredients except the salt. Stir to mix well.

2. Cook, uncovered, on the high heat setting about 2 hours, or until the nuts are toasted. Stir in the salt. Let cool. Store in an airtight container in the refrigerator up to 6 weeks. Serve at room temperature.

Chapter Two
Soups and Chowders

If you think long-cooking soups don't fit into your busy schedule, think again. The electric slow cooker can whip up a repertoire of delicious, soul-warming soups with a minimum of time, effort, and expense.

In mere minutes, with a contingent of pantry staples, such as chicken and beef broth, canned and dried beans, canned tomatoes, canned corn, and some frozen vegetables, you can get some of these soups on. No browning or precooking of ingredients is required here. Once everything is in the pot, you can walk away—in most cases until just prior to serving time.

The recipes in this chapter illustrate just how varied soups and chowders prepared in the slow cooker can be. Some are light, ideal for warm-weather days; others are hearty and make a satisfying meal-in-a-bowl, especially welcome on chilly nights. There are homey comforting soups and more sophisticated recipes that capitalize on chic new ingredients.

There's a hot asparagus soup that is pureed just prior to serving to lend it a thick consistency. It was so good, I couldn't stop eating it. The Butternut Squash Soup is also pureed after cooking and it has such a creamy consistency that it might even fool diners into thinking it contains cream.

To thicken slow-cooker soups, use flour, tomato paste, instant mashed potato flakes, and rice as specified in the recipes. Sometimes these ingredients are added at the beginning of the cooking time and in other instances at the end. To thicken bean soups more than prescribed, mash up or puree some of the liquid and beans in a blender or food processor, then stir back into the soup.

When using fish or shellfish in chowders and soups, they must be added near the end of the cooking time to preserve their delicate texture and subtle taste. Dairy products, such as heavy cream, milk, half-and-half, and sour cream, are also added near the end, to avoid separation. Individual recipes include specific instructions.

When making soups, the balance of seasonings is often a challenge. This is especially true for the slow cooker, because with lengthy simmering, seasonings and spices tend to dissipate or become diminished or diluted. That's why it's important to taste and correct seasonings before serving. In many instances, I add additional herbs and spices after the soup is finished cooking. By boosting these flavors you can avoid oversalting. Also, consider adding a splash of lemon, sherry or other wine, vinegar, or Worcestershire sauce to perk up a soup's flavor.

In most cases, I've included garnishes with the recipes. Soups tend to look bland, so a contrast of color really improves presentation. Some extra ideas for a soup garnish include pesto sauce, grated Parmesan cheese, salsa, chopped tomatoes or scallions, sliced radishes, chopped fresh cilantro or watercress, minced citrus zest, cubed avocado, toasted nuts or seeds, cooked whole shrimp, sliced olives, and sour cream or yogurt

Be sure to refrigerate or freeze any leftover soup within two hours so that you can warm it up for a fast lunch or dinner. Happily many soups taste even better a day or two later, after the flavors have had a chance to meld.

Fresh Asparagus Soup

When fresh asparagus is plentiful, whip up a pot of this full-flavored, rich-textured soup that is thickened by pureeing the vegetables. For best results when pureeing, add only a small amount of the cooking liquid to the vegetables.

MAKES 4 TO 5 SERVINGS

2 pounds fresh asparagus
5 cups homemade or canned chicken
   broth
4 scallions, chopped
2 medium russet potatoes, peeled and
   cut into ½-inch cubes

¼ teaspoon seasoned salt
¼ teaspoon freshly ground pepper
Sour cream or plain yogurt and
   chopped fresh tomatoes, for garnish

1. Break off the woody, fibrous ends of the asparagus spears and discard. Rinse the asparagus spears and cut into 1-inch pieces. Add to a 3½-quart electric slow cooker along with the broth, scallions, and potatoes.

2. Cover and cook on the low heat setting 6 to 7 hours, or until the potatoes are tender. Increase the heat to the high setting.

3. Using a blender or food processor, puree the vegetable solids in batches, with a little of the cooking liquid, until as smooth as possible. Return to the liquid remaining in the slow cooker. Stir in the seasoned salt and pepper. Cover and cook on high 30 minutes longer. Serve garnished with a dollop of sour cream or yogurt and chopped tomatoes.

NOTE: This soup can also be refrigerated and served cold.

Bean and Sausage Soup

Sausage lends hearty flavor to this Italian-flavored soup. For best results, add the sausage near the end of the cooking time, as indicated, just long enough to heat it through. For color, you can brown the sausage first in a skillet, if you like, and drain off the excess fat, but it isn't really necessary.

MAKES 4 TO 5 SERVINGS

1 cup dried small white beans, rinsed, drained, and picked over
1 (28-ounce) can diced peeled tomatoes
2 (14½-ounce) cans chicken broth
1 onion, chopped
2 garlic cloves, minced

1 (10-ounce) package frozen chopped spinach, thawed but not drained
1 tablespoon dried basil
½ teaspoon freshly ground pepper
½ pound turkey sausages, halved lengthwise and thinly sliced
Seasoned salt

1. In a 4- or 5-quart electric slow cooker, mix together the beans, tomatoes with their liquid, broth, onion, garlic, spinach, basil, and pepper.

2. Cover and cook on the low heat setting 8 to 9 hours, or until the beans are tender. Stir in the turkey sausages and add seasoned salt to taste. Cover and cook 30 minutes longer, or until the sausages are heated through.

Garbanzo Bean Soup

Make this hearty soup to warm chilly days and satisfy winter appetites. Serve it as a main dish and accompany it with garlic toast and fresh fruit.

MAKES 5 TO 6 SERVINGS

1 large onion, chopped
4 celery ribs, sliced
2 carrots, peeled and thinly sliced
2½ cups chopped green cabbage
(about ½ of a small head)
2 medium potatoes, peeled and cut
into ½-inch cubes
1½ cups chopped fresh tomatoes or 1
(14½-ounce) can diced peeled
tomatoes, drained
1 medium zucchini, diced
1 cup dried garbanzo beans (chick-peas),
rinsed, drained, and picked over

4 garlic cloves, minced
⅓ cup chopped fresh basil
1 bay leaf
½ teaspoon dried rosemary, crushed
½ teaspoon salt
¼ teaspoon ground pepper
3 (14½-ounce) cans chicken or vegetable broth
2 cups frozen cut green beans, thawed
¾ cup shredded or grated Parmesan
cheese

1. In a 5-quart electric slow cooker, mix together the onion, celery, carrots, cabbage, potatoes, tomatoes, zucchini, garbanzo beans, garlic, 3 tablespoons of the basil, the bay leaf, rosemary, salt, pepper, and chicken broth.

2. Cover and cook on the low heat setting about 8 hours, or until the beans are tender.

3. Remove the bay leaf. Stir in the green beans and remaining basil. Heat 10 to 15 minutes longer. Serve in soup bowls, topped with a generous sprinkling of cheese.

Beef Borscht

There are probably as many versions of borscht as there are cooks. I've adapted this rendition, enjoyed by my family, to the slow cooker with excellent success. Be sure to use well-trimmed beef to avoid fat in the finished soup. You can substitute canned julienned or diced beets for fresh; if you do so, stir them in with their liquid just before serving to retain good color. Accompany the borscht with dark bread for an easy supper.

MAKES 4 TO 6 SERVINGS

1 pound lean boneless beef chuck or beef top round steak, trimmed of fat and cut into ½- to ¾-inch cubes
4 cups water
1 (14½-ounce) can diced peeled tomatoes
1 large onion, chopped
4 large carrots, peeled and sliced
4 cups shredded green cabbage (½ of a small head)
1 (12-ounce) can tomato paste
½ teaspoon garlic powder
3 medium fresh beets, peeled and cut into ½-inch cubes
¾ teaspoon seasoned salt
¼ teaspoon freshly ground pepper
Sour cream or plain yogurt, for garnish

1. In a 5-quart electric slow cooker, mix together all the ingredients except the sour cream or yogurt.

2. Cover and cook on the low heat setting 7 to 8 hours, or until the meat is tender. Serve in soup bowls, topped with a dollop of sour cream or yogurt.

Beef Fajita Soup

This soup sizzles with the flavor of beef fajitas. To speed preparation time, I use a package of frozen fajita-style vegetables with strips of onions and red and green bell peppers already cut up.

MAKES 6 TO 8 SERVINGS

1 pound lean boneless beef stew meat, trimmed of all fat and cut into ½-inch cubes

1 (14½-ounce) can beef broth

2 cups water

1 (16-ounce) package frozen fajita-style vegetables, thawed

1 (14½-ounce) can Mexican-style thick and chunky tomato sauce

1 (15-ounce) can pinto beans, rinsed and drained

2 teaspoons ground cumin

1 (15-ounce) can black beans, rinsed and drained

¼ teaspoon seasoned salt

¼ teaspoon garlic pepper

Sour cream, chopped avocado, and shredded Monterey Jack or Cheddar cheese, for garnish

1. In a 3½-quart electric slow cooker, combine the beef, broth, water, vegetables, tomato sauce, pinto beans, and cumin.

2. Cover and cook on the low heat setting 8 to 8½ hours, or until the beef is tender.

3. Stir in the black beans, seasoned salt, and garlic pepper. Heat, covered, 10 minutes longer. Serve topped with sour cream, avocado, and cheese.

Butternut Squash Soup

This wonderful, subtle soup has a gorgeous bright golden hue. You'll be amazed at its creaminess and thickness once the cooked mixture is pureed.

MAKES 6 TO 8 SERVINGS

1 (2½-pound) butternut squash, halved, seeded, peeled, and cut into ¾- to 1-inch cubes

2 cups chopped leeks (white and light green part only)

2 large Granny Smith apples, peeled, cored, and diced

2 (14½-ounce) cans chicken broth

1 cup water

Seasoned salt and freshly ground white pepper

Chopped fresh parsley or chopped scallions, for garnish

1. In a 5-quart electric slow cooker, combine the squash, leeks, apples, broth, and water.

2. Cover and cook on the low heat setting 6 to 6½ hours, or until the squash and leeks are tender.

3. Increase the heat to the high setting. Carefully puree the hot soup in 3 or 4 batches in a food processor or blender until as smooth as possible. Return the pureed soup to the slow cooker.

4. Season with seasoned salt and white pepper to taste. Cover and cook on high ½ hour longer. Serve hot, garnished with a sprinkling of parsley or scallions.

Cabbage Soup with Rice and Dill

A flavorful soup that's hearty and filling. If you have any leftover cooked chicken, turkey, or ham, stir it in near the end of the cooking time for a meal-in-a-dish soup.

MAKES 7 TO 8 SERVINGS

1 medium head of green cabbage (about 1½ pounds), shredded (6 cups)

½ cup converted white rice

6 carrots, peeled and sliced

2 (14½-ounce) cans chicken broth

1 cup water

1 (15-ounce) can tomato sauce

1 tablespoon plus 1 teaspoon dried dill weed

½ teaspoon seasoned salt

¼ to ½ teaspoon freshly ground pepper

1 (14½-ounce) can diced peeled tomatoes

1. In a 4-quart electric slow cooker, mix together the cabbage, rice, carrots, broth, water, tomato sauce, 1 tablespoon of the dill weed, the seasoned salt, and pepper.

2. Cover and cook on the low heat setting 7 to 8 hours, or until the cabbage and rice are tender.

3. Stir in the tomatoes with their liquid and the remaining 1 teaspoon dill weed. Serve immediately.

Curried Cauliflower Soup

This delicious and unusual soup combines the flavors of curry, cumin, and tomato with cauliflower. If you like curry flavor and a tad of hotness, use the larger amount of curry. This is good served hot or cold.

MAKES 4 TO 5 SERVINGS

1 large head of cauliflower, separated
   into florets and chopped
1 (28-ounce) can diced peeled
   tomatoes
1 (14½-ounce) can vegetable or beef
   broth

1 medium onion, chopped
½ teaspoon garlic powder
2 to 2½ teaspoons Madras curry
   powder
⅛ teaspoon ground cumin
Salt and freshly ground pepper

1. In a 3½-quart electric slow cooker, combine the cauliflower, tomatoes with their liquid, broth, onion, and garlic powder.

2. Cover and cook on the low heat setting about 7 hours, or until the cauliflower is tender.

3. Increase the heat to the high setting. Stir in the curry powder and cumin and season with salt and pepper to taste. Cover and cook on high ½ hour longer. Serve hot or refrigerate and serve cold.

Caribbean Chicken Soup with Bananas

This substantial soup rates rave reviews with my two children and all who taste it. Everyone comes back for more. Be sure to make your own spice mixture and serve the soup over banana slices for tropical island flavor.

MAKES 6 TO 8 SERVINGS

1 medium onion, chopped
3 large carrots, peeled and thinly sliced
1 green bell pepper, cut into julienne strips
1 red bell pepper, cut into julienne strips
2 medium zucchini, halved lengthwise, then sliced
4 plum tomatoes, chopped

6 cups homemade chicken stock or 1 (49½-ounce) can chicken broth
1 (15¼-ounce) can whole kernel corn, drained
¾ cup converted white rice
Caribbean Spice Mix (recipe follows)
2 cups cooked chicken or turkey breast strips (about ½ pound)
3 bananas, thinly sliced

1. In a 6-quart electric slow cooker, combine the onion, carrots, green and red peppers, zucchini, tomatoes, stock, corn, rice, and spice mix. Stir to blend well.
2. Cover and cook on the low heat setting 6 to 7 hours, or until the rice is tender. Stir in the chicken or turkey. To serve, add almost one-half banana to each soup bowl. Ladle the soup over the bananas and serve at once.

CARIBBEAN SPICE MIX: In a small bowl, mix together 1 tablespoon paprika, 1 tablespoon chili powder, 1 tablespoon ground cumin, 1½ tablespoons dried thyme leaves, 1 teaspoon garlic salt, ½ teaspoon garlic powder, ¼ teaspoon Madras curry powder, ¼ teaspoon turmeric, ¼ teaspoon dried oregano, crumbled, and a pinch of cayenne.

Southwestern Chicken Soup

This delicious main-course soup flavored with corn, tomatoes, red and green peppers, and chicken breast strips is a breeze to make, thanks to several convenient canned items. Cumin, added at the end of the cooking time, gives the soup extra zip. Accompany the soup with a fruit salad and slices of peasant bread, and dinner is on.

MAKES 8 TO 10 SERVINGS

2 (14½-ounce) cans chicken broth
1 (14½-ounce) can diced peeled
    tomatoes
1 (4-ounce) can diced green chiles
1 (16-ounce) package frozen corn
    kernels, partially thawed
1 red bell pepper, chopped

1 green bell pepper, chopped
1 onion, chopped
4 skinless, boneless chicken breast
    halves, cut into thin strips
½ teaspoon garlic pepper
1 teaspoon ground cumin
Seasoned salt

1. In a 5-quart electric slow cooker, mix together the broth, tomatoes with their liquid, green chiles, corn, red and green peppers, onion, chicken strips, and garlic pepper.

2. Cover and cook on the high heat setting 1 hour. Reduce the heat to the low setting and continue cooking 3 to 4 hours, or until the chicken is cooked through and tender. Stir in the ground cumin and season with seasoned salt to taste. Serve immediately.

Buffalo Wing Soup with Pasta

This is an ideal soup to satisfy a hungry group while watching Sunday afternoon sports on TV. Serve it with celery sticks and blue cheese dip and wedges of corn bread.

MAKES 6 SERVINGS

1½ tablespoons paprika
1 tablespoon chili powder
1 tablespoon garlic powder
1 tablespoon garlic pepper
2 teaspoons dried oregano
1½ teaspoons ground cumin
1½ to 2 pounds chicken wing
   drumettes

2 (14½-ounce) cans chicken broth
1 (28-ounce) can diced peeled
   tomatoes
1 (7-ounce) can diced green chiles
1 red onion, diced
1½ teaspoons salt
8 ounces tubetti or other small pasta

1. In a bowl, mix together the paprika, chili powder, garlic powder, garlic pepper, oregano, and cumin until thoroughly blended. Add the chicken drumettes to the spice mixture and toss until completely coated. Set aside.

2. In a 4-quart electric slow cooker, combine the broth, tomatoes with their liquid, green chiles, red onion, and salt. Stir to combine. Push the drumettes down into the broth mixture and add any spice mixture remaining in the bowl. Cover and cook on the low heat setting 6 hours.

3. Turn the heat setting to high and stir in the pasta. Cover and cook on high 20 to 30 minutes, or until the pasta is tender but still firm.

Clam Chowder

Let the slow cooker tend to the cooking of this delicious chowder. Add the clams near the end of the cooking time so they won't become tough and lose their flavor. Stir in the half-and-half then, too.

MAKES 4 TO 5 SERVINGS

1 onion, chopped

2 celery ribs, sliced

2 ounces pancetta or lean bacon, finely diced

¼ cup all-purpose flour

1½ cups cold water

1¼ pounds russet baking potatoes (about 4 medium), peeled and cut into small cubes

¾ teaspoon dried thyme leaves

2 (6½-ounce) cans chopped or minced clams

2 cups half-and-half

¼ to ½ teaspoon seasoned salt

¼ teaspoon freshly ground pepper

Chopped fresh parsley, for garnish

1. In a 3½-quart electric slow cooker, combine the onion, celery, and pancetta.

2. Whisk the flour into ½ cup of the cold water. Stir into the vegetables in the slow cooker. Stir in the remaining 1 cup water and add the potatoes and thyme.

3. Drain the liquid from the clams into the slow cooker; reserve the clams in the refrigerator.

4. Cover and cook on the low heat setting about 6 hours, stirring once or twice, if possible, until the potatoes are tender, but not mushy and falling apart.

5. Increase the heat setting to high. Stir in the reserved clams, half-and-half, seasoned salt, and pepper. Cook, uncovered, on high 30 to 40 minutes, stirring occasionally. Serve hot, garnished with a sprinkling of parsley.

Lentil-Red Pepper Soup

Here's a zesty twist on traditional lentil soup. For convenience, I use jarred roasted red peppers to make the puree that goes into the soup, but you can roast a large pepper if you prefer. To add a colorful garnish, top with some diced roasted red peppers and a dollop of sour cream.

MAKES 6 TO 8 SERVINGS

1 (16-ounce) package lentils, rinsed, drained, and picked over
2 medium onions, chopped
2 large carrots, chopped
1 ham hock
5 cups homemade chicken stock or 3 (14½-ounce) cans chicken broth
2 cups water

1 to 1½ teaspoons ground cumin
⅛ teaspoon cayenne
1 (4-ounce) can diced green chiles
1 cup roasted red peppers, rinsed, drained, and pureed in a food processor
Salt

1. In a 5-quart electric slow cooker, mix together the lentils, onions, carrots, ham hock, stock, and water.

2. Cover and cook on the low heat setting 9 hours, or until the lentils are tender. Remove the ham hock; finely chop the meat and return it to the slow cooker. Discard the bone. Stir in the cumin, cayenne, green chiles, and red pepper puree. Season with salt to taste. Increase the heat to the high setting and cook 15 minutes longer.

Minestrone

This versatile version of the Italian favorite is filled with plenty of good flavor. To make it even more substantial, add a can of rinsed and drained cannellini beans just before serving.

MAKES 6 TO 8 SERVINGS

6 cups homemade chicken or beef
   stock or 1 (49½-ounce) can
   chicken or beef broth
1 (28-ounce) can diced peeled
   tomatoes
2 cups sliced carrots (5 or 6 medium)
½ pound fresh green beans, cut into
   1-inch pieces
3 large celery ribs, sliced
1 large onion, chopped

¾ pound red potatoes, scrubbed and
   cut into ½-inch dice
1 tablespoon dried basil
2 teaspoons dried Italian seasoning
2 garlic cloves, crushed through a
   press
¼ cup chopped fresh basil
1 tablespoon extra-virgin olive oil
Salt and garlic pepper
Grated Parmesan cheese

1. In a 6-quart electric slow cooker, mix together the stock, tomatoes with their liquid, carrots, green beans, celery, onion, potatoes, dried basil, Italian seasoning, and garlic.

2. Cover and cook on the low heat setting about 8 hours, or until the potatoes are tender. Stir in the fresh basil and olive oil. Season with salt and garlic pepper to taste. Pass a bowl of grated Parmesan cheese on the side.

Potato Leek Soup

Because dairy products tend to break down during long, slow cooking, add the heavy cream just before serving. Leeks, potatoes, and dill weed have an affinity for one another, as this soup attests.

MAKES 5 TO 6 SERVINGS

2 pounds potatoes (about 5 to 6 medium), peeled and cut into ¾-inch cubes

3 tablespoons all-purpose flour

5 cups homemade or canned chicken broth

2 medium leeks (white and tender green), rinsed well and chopped

6 tablespoons chopped fresh dill or 2½ tablespoons dried dill weed

1 to 1½ cups chopped cooked ham or 1½ cups cooked, shelled, and deveined shrimp

¾ cup heavy cream

1. Place the potatoes in a 4-quart electric slow cooker. Sprinkle on the flour and toss well. Add the chicken broth, mixing well. Stir in the leeks and 3 tablespoons of the fresh dill or 1½ tablespoons of the dried.

2. Cover and cook on the low heat setting 8 to 8½ hours, or until the potatoes are tender. In a blender or a food processor, puree 1 to 2 cups of the potatoes and leeks with a little of the soup liquid and return to the soup remaining in the slow cooker. Stir in the ham, cream, and remaining 3 tablespoons fresh dill or 1 tablespoon dried. Cover and heat 5 to 10 minutes longer. Serve immediately.

Curried Pumpkin Bisque

Heavy cream, milk, and mushrooms are stirred in at the end of the cooking time for body and texture.

MAKES 8 TO 10 SERVINGS

1 (29-ounce) can solid-pack pumpkin
4 cups homemade or canned chicken
 broth
2 medium onions, chopped
2 garlic cloves, crushed through a
 press
1½ tablespoons Madras curry powder
½ teaspoon seasoned salt

1 cup heavy cream
½ cup milk
½ teaspoon sugar
1 or 2 (4½-ounce) cans mushroom
 stems and pieces, well drained
Sour cream and chopped scallions or
 crisp bacon bits, for garnish

1. In a 3½-quart electric slow cooker, mix together the pumpkin, broth, onions, garlic, curry powder, and seasoned salt.

2. Cover and cook on the high heat setting 3 to 3½ hours. Carefully puree the hot soup in 2 or 3 batches in a blender or food processor until as smooth as possible. Return to the slow cooker.

3. Stir in the cream, milk, sugar, and mushrooms. Cover and cook on high 15 to 30 minutes longer. Serve immediately in soup bowls garnished with sour cream and scallions or bacon bits.

Sauerkraut Tomato Soup

This beef-based sweet-and-sour soup has a wonderful old-world flavor. Serve with plenty of dark bread for a meal-in-one dish. Stash any leftover soup in the fridge; it's delicious a day or two later.

MAKES 6 TO 8 SERVINGS

2 pounds sauerkraut, rinsed and drained

1 (28-ounce) can diced peeled tomatoes

5 cups water

1 (6-ounce) can tomato paste

2 bay leaves

¼ teaspoon freshly ground pepper, or more to taste

¼ teaspoon seasoned salt, or more to taste

1½ pounds lean beef sirloin or beef top round steak, trimmed of fat and cut into ½-inch cubes

2½ tablespoons sugar

3 tablespoons fresh lemon juice

1. In a 5- or 6-quart electric slow cooker, combine the sauerkraut, tomatoes with their liquid, water, tomato paste, bay leaves, pepper, seasoned salt, and beef.

2. Cover and cook on the high heat setting 3 hours. Reduce the heat to the low setting and continue cooking, covered, 3½ hours longer, or until the beef is tender.

3. Remove and discard the bay leaves. Stir in the sugar, lemon juice, and more seasoned salt and pepper to taste, if you feel it needs it. Serve immediately.

Seafood, Potato, and Corn Chowder

Add the fish at the end of the cooking time to avoid overcooking it. Serve this hearty chowder as a main course, accompanied by a tossed green salad and bruschetta.

MAKES 4 TO 6 SERVINGS

1 (49½-ounce) can chicken broth

1 onion, chopped

2 large potatoes (about 1¼ pounds), peeled and cut into ½-inch dice

1 (15¼-ounce) can whole kernel corn, well drained

¼ cup all-purpose flour

2 tablespoons dried dill weed

½ cup heavy cream

½ pound firm-fleshed white fish, such as halibut, cut into ½-inch dice

½ pound cooked, shelled, and deveined medium shrimp

¼ teaspoon garlic pepper

⅔ cup instant mashed potato buds

Salt

1. In a 3½-quart electric slow cooker, combine the broth, onion, potatoes, corn, flour, and 5 teaspoons of the dill weed.

2. Cover and cook on the low heat setting about 5½ hours, or until the potatoes are just barely tender. Increase the heat setting to high. Stir in the remaining 1 teaspoon dill weed, cream, white fish, shrimp, garlic pepper, and potato buds. Cover and cook on high 35 to 45 minutes longer, or until slightly thickened. Season with salt to taste.

Shrimp and Rice Soup with Chipotle Chile

The smoky flavor of chipotle chiles contained in a can of salsa gives this colorful soup its hot and spicy flavor. If this style salsa is too hot for you, tone down the recipe by using a milder one. If you do so, to avoid missing out on the smoky flavor that comes from the chipotles, add a few dashes of liquid smoke seasoning.

MAKES 6 SERVINGS

6 cups homemade chicken stock or 1 (49½-ounce) can chicken broth
1 (14½-ounce) can hot salsa with chipotle peppers, diced tomatoes, onions, garlic, and spices
¾ cup converted white rice
1 medium onion, chopped

1 (16-ounce) package frozen fajita-style vegetables with black beans, thawed
1 pound cooked, shelled, and deveined medium shrimp
½ teaspoon salt
2 tablespoons fresh lemon juice
3 tablespoons chopped fresh cilantro

1. In a 3½- or 4-quart electric slow cooker, combine the stock, salsa, rice, and onion.
2. Cover and cook on the low heat setting about 3½ hours, or until the rice is tender but not mushy. Increase the heat to the high setting.
3. Stir in the vegetables, shrimp, and salt and cook on high until the shrimp and vegetables are hot, about 15 to 20 minutes longer. Stir in the lemon juice. Ladle into soup bowls and sprinkle the cilantro on top.

Curried Split Pea Soup

Zip up the flavor of traditional split pea soup with curry powder. Give the soup an added flavor boost at the end of the cooking time by stirring in a little additional spice.

MAKES 6 TO 8 SERVINGS

1 (16-ounce) package dried green split peas, rinsed, drained, and picked over
1 medium onion, chopped
6 cups boiling water
2½ tablespoons Madras curry powder
6 carrots, peeled and chopped

2 celery ribs, chopped
¼ teaspoon seasoned salt, or more to taste
¼ teaspoon freshly ground pepper, or more to taste
1 cup chopped Canadian bacon

1. In a 4- or 5-quart electric slow cooker, mix together all the ingredients except ½ tablespoon of the curry powder.

2. Cover and cook on the low heat setting 9 to 10 hours. Stir in the remaining ½ tablespoon curry powder. Add more seasoned salt and pepper to taste, if needed.

Tortellini and Vegetable Soup

This is a favorite with both adults and children—and it couldn't be simpler. Serve topped with grated Parmesan cheese.

MAKES 4 TO 5 SERVINGS

2 (14½-ounce) cans vegetable broth

1 (15¼-ounce) can whole kernel corn, drained

1 medium leek (white and tender green), rinsed well and chopped

2 garlic cloves, crushed through a press

¼ cup chopped fresh basil

1 (28-ounce) can diced peeled tomatoes

1 red bell pepper, chopped

2 cups chopped zucchini (about 1 medium)

1 (9-ounce) package fresh cheese tortellini

½ teaspoon garlic pepper

Grated Parmesan cheese, for serving

1. In a 4-quart electric slow cooker, mix together all the ingredients except the grated cheese.

2. Cover and cook on the high heat setting 3½ to 4 hours, or until the tortellini are tender. Do not overcook or the tortellini will become mushy. Serve immediately, topped with a sprinkling of cheese.

Tarragon Turkey Soup with Corn and Rice

Here's a good way to use up leftover turkey or chicken. Tarragon lends its distinctive grassy, aniselike taste to this soup. If you've never tried the herb, this recipe offers a good way to acquaint yourself with it.

MAKES 4 TO 6 SERVINGS

6 cups homemade chicken stock or 1 (49½-ounce) can chicken broth
1 (16-ounce) package frozen whole kernel corn
½ cup converted white rice
2 large celery ribs, chopped
1 medium onion, chopped
1 small green bell pepper, chopped
1 small red bell pepper, chopped
2 tablespoons plus 2 teaspoons dried tarragon, crushed
2 cups chopped cooked turkey or chicken (about ½ pound)
Salt and freshly ground pepper

1. In a 4-quart electric slow cooker, mix together the stock, corn, rice, celery, onion, green and red bell peppers, and 2 tablespoons of the tarragon.

2. Cover and cook on the low heat setting 5 to 5½ hours, or until the rice is tender. Stir in the turkey or chicken.

3. Season with salt and pepper to taste. Stir in the remaining 2 teaspoons tarragon. Cook 30 to 45 minutes longer.

Fresh Vegetable Soup with Garbanzo Beans

Use this as a base to make vegetable soup. Vary the fresh produce according to what's in season, in your garden, or stashed in your refrigerator vegetable bin.

MAKES 5 TO 6 SERVINGS

2 medium zucchini, chopped
1 medium onion, chopped
3 celery ribs, chopped
2 cups shredded carrots (about 3 medium-large)
1 cup cut-up fresh green beans
2 plum tomatoes, chopped
2 garlic cloves, crushed through a press
3 tablespoons chopped fresh parsley
¼ cup chopped fresh basil

½ teaspoon seasoned salt
½ teaspoon freshly ground pepper
2 (14½-ounce) cans beef or chicken broth
1 (14½-ounce) can diced peeled tomatoes
1 (15½-ounce) can garbanzo beans (chick-peas), rinsed and drained
½ cup grated imported Parmesan cheese

1. In a 4-quart electric slow cooker, mix together all the ingredients except the grated cheese.

2. Cover and cook on the low heat setting 5 to 6 hours, or until the vegetables are tender but still firm. Ladle into soup bowls and top with a sprinkling of cheese.

Simple Vegetable Soup

This light soup is a great pick-me-up any time of day for those watching their fat intake or counting calories.

3 cups chopped leeks, white and light green part only (about 2 medium leeks)

2 cups diced carrots (about 3 large)

3 cups diced unpeeled zucchini (about 2½ medium)

2 (14½-ounce) cans vegetable broth

1 cup water

¼ teaspoon salt

⅛ teaspoon freshly ground pepper

3 plum tomatoes, chopped

1. In a 3½-quart electric slow cooker, mix together the leeks, carrots, zucchini, broth, water, salt, and pepper.

2. Cover and cook on the low heat setting 5½ to 6 hours, or until the vegetables are tender.

3. Carefully transfer 3 cups of the vegetables with a little of their cooking liquid to a blender or food processor and puree until as smooth as possible. Return to the soup remaining in the slow cooker and mix well. Serve hot, garnished with chopped tomatoes.

Chapter Three
Chilis and Stews

For making chilis and stews, a slow cooker can't be beat. It is a natural for melding a wide array of seasonings and flavorings and infusing them into various meats and vegetables.

The preparation and cooking of chilis and stews is so easy and effortless because everything goes into a single pot. The recipes here range from fiery and mild "bowls of red" to ethnic-inspired stews from around the world. These are the comforting dishes that I rely on when my time is required elsewhere and I need to get something into the slow cooker and get myself out of the kitchen fast. They all go together in a jiffy.

There are all kinds of chilis in this chapter, simply designed for good eating. Some are traditional; others such as Spicy Pineapple Pork Chili, White Bean Turkey Chili, Pork-Tomatillo Chili, and Turkey and Black-Eyed Pea Chili, provide more adventurous fare.

In the stew realm, there are classic meat and vegetable stews that may stir up childhood memories as well as some offbeat interpretations on the theme: Curried Beef and Potato Stew, Fisherman's Stew, Chicken Stew Mexican Style, Veal Stew with Green Olives, Greek-inspired Beef Stifado, and a Chinese Beef and Vegetable Stew.

If the consistency of a finished chili or stew isn't just as you like it, add extra stock or a little water to thin the sauce or for a thicker mélange, remove the slow cooker lid and cook, uncovered, on high 30 minutes longer, to evaporate some of the excess liquid. Sometimes I stir in some of the tomato paste or barbecue sauce near the end to help thicken the stew.

The chilis are good served over rice or in some cases simply with a side of corn bread. You can also turn them into other dishes by serving them wrapped in tortillas as burritos or using them as a base for tostadas and piling them high with lettuce, vegetables, and shredded cheeses. You might want to accompany the stews with a spinach or tossed salad and some crusty bread or rolls.

Red Bean Beef Chili

Whether you are serving the dish at home or carrying it to a potluck party, the electric slow cooker is perfect for chili. Vary the amount of chili powder to suit your taste. For spicier chili, use the larger quantity.

MAKES 6 TO 8 SERVINGS

1 pound lean ground beef

1 large onion, chopped

1 (16-ounce) package dried small red beans, rinsed, drained, and picked over

1 (16-ounce) jar roasted red peppers, rinsed, drained, and coarsely chopped

1 (28-ounce) can diced peeled tomatoes

1 (15-ounce) can tomato sauce

3 to 4 tablespoons chili powder, preferably New Mexico chili powder

1½ tablespoons ground cumin

1 teaspoon garlic powder

Shredded Monterey Jack or Cheddar cheese, chopped onions, chopped tomatoes, and sour cream, for serving

1. In a large skillet, cook the beef and onion over medium-high heat, stirring, until the beef is browned, 6 to 8 minutes. Drain off any fat. Turn into a 5-quart electric slow cooker. Add the beans, red peppers, tomatoes with their liquid, tomato sauce, chili powder, cumin, and garlic powder. Mix well.

2. Cover and cook on the low heat setting 9 to 10 hours, or until the beans are tender. Serve topped with cheese, onions, tomatoes, and sour cream, as desired.

Easy Beef Chili

This is a cinch to prepare with a little assistance from canned beans, tomatoes, and green chiles. Use it as a base for tostada salads or as a filling for tacos or burritos.

MAKES 5 TO 6 SERVINGS

1 pound boneless beef round steak, trimmed of all fat and cut into ½-inch cubes
1½ tablespoons ground cumin
2 tablespoons chili powder
½ teaspoon seasoned salt
3 garlic cloves, crushed through a press
1 (7-ounce) can diced green chiles

1 medium onion, chopped
1 (30-ounce) can chili beans, undrained
2 (15-ounce) cans black beans, rinsed and drained
1 (14½-ounce) can diced peeled tomatoes
1 (12-ounce) can or 2 (6-ounce) cans tomato paste

1. In a 4- or 5-quart electric slow cooker, mix together the beef, cumin, chili powder, seasoned salt, garlic, chiles, and onion. Add the chili beans, black beans, tomatoes with their liquid, and tomato paste. Mix gently to avoid smashing the beans.

2. Cover and cook on the low heat setting about 5 hours, or until the beef is tender.

Italian-Style Beef Stew

For a change of pace, leave out the white beans and serve this saucy mixture over hot cooked pasta.

MAKES 6 TO 8 SERVINGS

2 pounds lean boneless beef stew meat, trimmed of fat and cut into 1-inch cubes

3 ounces prosciutto, chopped

1 large onion, chopped

2 (14½-ounce) cans diced Italian-style tomatoes (with Italian seasonings)

2 (6-ounce) cans tomato paste

1 cup dry white wine

1½ tablespoons dried basil

3 garlic cloves, crushed through a press

1 fennel bulb, chopped

1 (15-ounce) can cannellini beans (white kidney beans), rinsed and drained

Pinch of sugar

1 teaspoon salt

½ teaspoon freshly ground pepper

1. In a 4-quart electric slow cooker, mix together the beef, prosciutto, onion, tomatoes with their liquid, tomato paste, wine, basil, garlic, and fennel.

2. Cover and cook on the low heat setting 8½ to 9 hours, or until the beef is tender but not mushy. Stir in the beans, sugar, salt, and pepper.

Chinese Beef and Vegetable Stew

Chinese flavorings and a mix of Asian and ordinary vegetables give this stew a contemporary East-West twist. Serve over hot steamed rice.

MAKES 5 TO 6 SERVINGS

4 cups (packed) shredded Napa
   cabbage
1 green bell pepper, cut into thin 1½-
   inch-long strips
1 (4½-ounce) jar sliced mushrooms,
   rinsed and drained
6 scallions, chopped
1 (8-ounce) can sliced water chestnuts,
   drained
1 pound beef top round steak, cut
   across the grain into thin strips
¼ cup dry sherry

3 tablespoons soy sauce
3 tablespoons water
3 tablespoons hoisin sauce
1 to 1½ teaspoons Chinese chili paste
   with garlic
½ teaspoon garlic powder
¼ teaspoon garlic pepper
1½ tablespoons cornstarch
1 (16-ounce) package frozen cut
   young green beans, thawed
½ red bell pepper, chopped

1. In a 3½- or 4-quart electric slow cooker, mix together the cabbage, green pepper, mushrooms, scallions, water chestnuts, and beef. In a small bowl, mix together 2 tablespoons each of the sherry and soy sauce, the water, hoisin sauce, chili paste with garlic, and garlic powder. Pour over the beef and vegetables in the pot. Sprinkle with the garlic pepper.

2. Cover and cook on the low heat setting 5½ to 6 hours. In a small bowl or cup, mix together the cornstarch and remaining 2 tablespoons sherry and 1 tablespoon soy sauce. Increase the heat setting to high. Stir in the cornstarch mixture. Place the cover slightly ajar and cook on high ½ hour, stirring once or twice, until the sauce clears and thickens slightly. Stir in the green beans and red pepper and cook 5 to 10 minutes longer.

NOTE: Use a 4-quart slow cooker and stir in 1 to 2 cups bean sprouts along with the cabbage, if desired.

Layered Potato, Sauerkraut, and Beef Stew

Serve this stew with old-world flavor with plenty of dark bread and a spinach or other green salad.

MAKES 5 TO 6 SERVINGS

1 pound small white potatoes, scrubbed and sliced

2 pounds sauerkraut, rinsed and drained

1 medium onion, halved and thinly sliced

¼ cup dry white wine

2 tablespoons cornstarch

1 (14½-ounce) can diced peeled tomatoes

½ teaspoon garlic pepper

¼ teaspoon salt

1 tablespoon caraway seeds (optional)

2 pounds beef top round steak, trimmed of fat and cut into 1-inch cubes

1. In a 5-quart electric slow cooker, layer the potato slices. Spread evenly with the sauerkraut, then top with the onion slices. In a medium bowl, blend together the wine and cornstarch until smooth. Stir in the tomatoes with their liquid, garlic pepper, salt, and caraway seeds. Pour ⅔ of the tomato mixture over the potatoes and sauerkraut. Top with the beef cubes. Pour the remaining tomato mixture over all.

2. Cover and cook on the low heat setting about 9 hours, or until the beef and potatoes are tender. Serve immediately.

Beef Stifado

This is an updated, slow-cooker version of a classic Greek stew. Cinnamon, cumin, and lemon give it a complex, immensely appealing flavor. Serve with rice or noodles and steamed or braised spinach or other greens tossed with olive oil, lemon juice, and garlic.

MAKES 6 SERVINGS

1¾ to 2 pounds boneless beef top round steak, cut into 1-inch cubes or sliced in thin strips across the grain
2 tablespoons all-purpose flour
2 large onions, halved, each half cut in 8 thin wedges
1 (6-ounce) can tomato paste

½ cup dry red wine
½ teaspoon ground cumin
½ teaspoon ground cinnamon
3 tablespoons lemon juice
2 tablespoons water
½ teaspoon sugar
⅓ cup chopped walnuts
½ cup crumbled feta cheese

1. In a 3½-quart electric slow cooker, toss the beef with the flour until evenly coated. Mix in the onions.

2. In a small bowl, stir together the tomato paste, red wine, cumin, cinnamon, lemon juice, and water until well blended. Stir into the beef mixture in the slow cooker.

3. Cover and cook on the low heat setting 6 to 7 hours, or until the meat is tender, but not falling apart. Stir in the sugar. Serve topped with the walnuts and feta cheese.

Curried Beef and Potato Stew

This appealing stew blends the curry and the chutney all in one pot. Stir in the green peas near the end of the cooking time so they keep their appealing color.

MAKES 4 TO 6 SERVINGS

2 pounds lean boneless beef stew meat, trimmed of fat and cut into 1-inch cubes

2 pounds red potatoes, peeled and cut into ¾-inch pieces

1 medium onion, chopped

¾ cup mango chutney or Dried Fruit Chutney (page 176)

¼ cup raisins

3 tablespoons quick-mixing flour, such as Wondra

1 cup water

1 teaspoon beef bouillon granules

1½ to 2 tablespoons Madras curry powder

½ teaspoon ground ginger

½ teaspoon garlic powder

¼ teaspoon freshly ground pepper

¼ teaspoon salt

2 cups frozen green peas, thawed

1. In a 4- or 5-quart electric slow cooker, mix together all the ingredients except the peas.

2. Cover and cook on the low heat setting 7 to 8 hours, or until the beef and potatoes are tender but not falling apart, stirring once during the cooking time, if possible.

3. Stir in the peas, cover, and cook 15 minutes longer.

Beef and Vegetable Stew

This is a good old-fashioned basic beef stew. No prebrowning is required. Toss everything in the slow cooker and 8 to 9 hours later, the stew is ready to serve.

MAKES 6 SERVINGS

6 medium russet potatoes (about 2 pounds), peeled and cubed

6 medium carrots, peeled and cut diagonally into ¼-inch slices

1 onion, coarsely chopped

1 celery rib, chopped

2 pounds lean boneless beef stew meat or boneless beef cross rib roast, trimmed of fat and cut into 1-inch cubes

3 tablespoons all-purpose flour

1 (14½-ounce) can diced peeled tomatoes

1 cup dry red wine

1 teaspoon dry mustard

1 teaspoon dried thyme leaves

½ teaspoon freshly ground pepper

Salt

1. In a 6-quart electric slow cooker, mix the potatoes, carrots, onion, and celery. Toss the beef with the flour to coat evenly. Add to the slow cooker. Top with the tomatoes with their liquid mixed with the red wine, dry mustard, thyme, and pepper.

2. Cover and cook on the high heat setting 1 to 1½ hours. Reduce the heat setting to low and cook 7 to 8 hours longer, or until the beef is tender, stirring once or twice during cooking, if possible. Season with salt to taste.

Winter Beef Stew with Apricots and Prunes

Beer, brandy, sweet spices, and dried fruits create a rich, dark, savory one-pot meal appropriate for entertaining. Serve with crusty bread and a tossed salad on the side.

MAKES 6 TO 7 SERVINGS

1 (12-ounce) bottle dark beer
½ cup brandy
2 tablespoons Worcestershire sauce
¼ cup orange marmalade
1 tablespoon ground cinnamon
1½ teaspoons grated nutmeg
½ teaspoon ground ginger
1 teaspoon salt
½ teaspoon freshly ground pepper
½ cup quick-mixing flour, such as Wondra
4 medium russet potatoes (about 1¼ pounds), peeled and cut into 1-inch cubes

2 sweet potatoes (about 1 pound), peeled and cut into 1-inch cubes
2 onions, sliced and separated into rings
4 carrots, peeled and cut into ½-inch slices
¾ cup dried apricots
¾ cup pitted prunes
1 (2½- to 3-pound) boneless beef chuck shoulder roast, trimmed of fat

1. In a 6-quart electric slow cooker, mix together the beer, brandy, Worcestershire sauce, marmalade, cinnamon, nutmeg, ginger, salt, pepper, and flour. Reserve ½ to ¾ cup of this beer mixture. To the mixture remaining in the slow cooker, add the potatoes, sweet potatoes, onions, carrots, apricots, and prunes; mix well. Cut the beef in half horizontally so you end up with 2 pieces, each about 1½ inches thick. Add to the slow cooker. Evenly pour the reserved beer mixture over the top.

2. Cover and cook on the low heat setting 10 to 11 hours, or until the beef and potatoes are tender, stirring once during the cooking time, if possible. Taste and season with more cinnamon and nutmeg, if desired.

Lamb and Lima Bean Stew

Lamb and beans are a wonderful pairing. With its herbs, wine, and tomatoes, this savory stew has Mediterranean overtones. Feta cheese crumbled over the top with a sprinkling of chopped fresh parsley makes it appealing looking as well.

MAKES 5 TO 6 SERVINGS

1 (16-ounce) package dried baby lima beans, rinsed, drained, and picked over
2 medium onions, chopped
2 garlic cloves, minced
1 (14½-ounce) can diced peeled tomatoes
¾ cup dry white wine
2 cups water
1 teaspoon dried marjoram

1 teaspoon dry mustard
⅓ cup chopped fresh parsley
2 lemons—grated zest from 1, juice from 2
1 tablespoon olive oil
2½ pounds boneless lamb stew meat, trimmed of all fat and cut into 1½-inch cubes
¾ to 1 cup crumbled feta cheese

1. In a 4-quart electric slow cooker, mix together the lima beans, onions, garlic, tomatoes with their liquid, wine, 1 cup of the water, the marjoram, mustard, 3 tablespoons of the parsley, and the lemon zest; mix well. In a large skillet, heat the olive oil over high heat until hot. Add half of the lamb and cook, stirring often, until well browned, 5 to 7 minutes. With a slotted spoon, transfer the lamb to the slow cooker, layering it over the bean mixture. Repeat with the remaining lamb.

2. Pour out any fat in the pan. Add the remaining 1 cup water to the skillet and bring to a boil, scraping up any brown bits from the bottom of the pan. Mix well. Scrape the mixture into the slow cooker and mix well.

3. Cover and cook on the low heat setting 7 to 8 hours, or until the beans are just tender. Do not overcook, or the beans will become mushy. Just before serving, squeeze the juice from the lemons over the stew. Sprinkle the top of each serving with a little of the feta cheese and the remaining parsley.

Veal Stew with Green Olives

This dish is redolent with lemon and sparked with capers and green olives. Serve over hot cooked pasta or rice.

MAKES 4 TO 6 SERVINGS

2 pounds boneless veal stew meat, trimmed of fat and cut into 1½-inch cubes
⅓ cup all-purpose flour
1 onion, chopped
1½ cups chopped carrots (3 or 4 medium)
2 tomatoes, chopped

2 garlic cloves, minced
¾ cup rinsed and chopped pimiento-stuffed green olives
Grated zest and juice of 1 lemon
½ teaspoon dried rosemary, crumbled
1 cup dry white wine
¾ cup chicken broth
2 tablespoons drained capers

1. In a 3½-quart electric slow cooker, toss the veal cubes with the flour until evenly coated. Add the onion, carrots, tomatoes, garlic, olives, lemon zest, rosemary, wine, and broth. Mix well.

2. Cover and cook on the low heat setting 6 to 6½ hours, or until the veal is tender. Just before serving, stir in the capers and lemon juice.

Spicy Pineapple Pork Chili

This spicy chili has a surprise: pineapple chunks that add a refreshing note of coolness to the heat. Reduce the amount of chiles for a less spicy stew.

MAKES 4 TO 6 SERVINGS

1 pound lean boneless pork, trimmed of fat and cut into 1-inch cubes

1 cup dried small white beans, rinsed, drained, and picked over

1 cup hot water

1 (14½-ounce) can diced tomatoes in puree

1 (6-ounce) can tomato paste

1 (20-ounce) can unsweetened pineapple chunks, drained, juice reserved

1 (4-ounce) can diced green chiles

1 medium onion, chopped

1 tablespoon chili powder

1 tablespoon ground cumin

½ teaspoon garlic powder

1. In a 3½-quart electric slow cooker, combine the pork, beans, hot water, tomatoes with their liquid, tomato paste, juice drained from the pineapple chunks, chiles, onion, chili powder, cumin, and garlic powder. Mix well.

2. Cover and cook on the low heat setting 8½ to 9 hours, until the pork and beans are tender, stirring once halfway through the cooking time, if possible. Stir in the pineapple chunks and serve.

Pork-Tomatillo Chili

Tomatillos, which resemble small green tomatoes in size and shape and have a lemon-herblike, acidic flavor, are used in this interesting chili. Purchase firm fruit with tight-fitting parchmentlike or papery husks and remove the husks and rinse the fruit before using. Serve over hot cooked rice, garnished with lime wedges, avocado slices, and sour cream.

MAKES 6 SERVINGS

2 tablespoons vegetable oil

2 pounds lean boneless pork, trimmed of fat and cut into 1-inch cubes

Salt and freshly ground pepper

2 medium onions, thinly sliced and separated into rings

⅓ cup frozen orange juice concentrate, thawed

1 (12-ounce) bottle dark beer

2 garlic cloves, crushed through a press

1 jalapeño pepper, seeded and finely diced

½ cup chopped fresh cilantro

1 (14½-ounce) can diced peeled tomatoes, well drained

4 plum tomatoes, chopped

1 (15-ounce) can black beans, rinsed and drained

1 pound fresh tomatillos, husks removed and discarded, cored and cut into 6 wedges each

1. In a large skillet, heat the oil until hot. Add half of the pork cubes and cook over medium-high heat, stirring often, until the pork is well browned all over, 6 to 8 minutes. (Cover skillet as necessary.) Season with salt and pepper to taste. Turn the browned pork into a 4- to 5-quart electric slow cooker. Repeat with the remaining pork; turn into the slow cooker.

2. Add the onions, orange juice concentrate, beer, garlic, jalapeño pepper, cilantro, drained canned tomatoes, chopped fresh tomatoes, beans, and tomatillos to the slow cooker. Stir to mix well.

3. Cover and cook on the low heat setting 6 to 7 hours, or until the pork is tender.

Pork and Squash Stew

This stew is aromatic and delicious with chunks of pork and yellow squash in a sauce prepared with red wine, cinnamon, and nutmeg.

MAKES 4 TO 5 SERVINGS

1½ pounds hubbard or banana squash, skinned and cut into 1-inch cubes
1 medium onion, sliced
1 cup dry red wine
1 tablespoon Worcestershire sauce
3 tablespoons raisins
2 tablespoons brown sugar
1½ teaspoons ground cinnamon
¼ teaspoon grated nutmeg
¼ cup water
3 tablespoons quick-mixing flour, such as Wondra
1½ pounds lean boneless pork cubes, trimmed of fat and cut into 1-inch cubes
Chopped fresh parsley, for garnish

1. In a 4-quart electric slow cooker, mix together all the ingredients except the parsley.

2. Cover and cook on the low heat setting 8½ to 9 hours, or until the pork and squash are tender but not falling apart, stirring once halfway through the cooking time, if possible. Serve immediately, garnished with chopped parsley.

Posole

Posole is a humble Aztec stew containing white hominy and chiles. The flavors of the spicy broth with pork, chicken, and hominy give this version a unique earthy character. Serve in large shallow soup plates, garnished with chopped raw vegetables and lime wedges to squeeze into the stew.

MAKES 6 TO 8 SERVINGS

3 dried mild red chiles, such as New Mexico or ancho

2 pounds center-cut pork loin, trimmed of fat and cut into 1½-inch cubes

1 pound skinless, boneless chicken breast tenders

4 cups homemade or canned chicken broth

1 onion, diced

1 (7-ounce) can diced green chiles

2 (15-ounce) cans white hominy, rinsed and drained

7 garlic cloves, minced

1 tablespoon chili powder

2 teaspoons dried oregano

2 teaspoons ground cumin

1 teaspoon salt

Chopped scallions, chopped cilantro, shredded green cabbage, shredded red radishes, and fresh lime juice, for garnish

1. Remove the stems from the dried chiles, rinse well, and remove the seeds. Soak in hot water to cover for 10 minutes to soften. Drain, discarding the soaking water. Cut the chiles into strips.

2. In a 5-quart electric slow cooker, mix together the pork cubes, whole chicken tenders, broth, onion, green chiles, hominy, garlic, chili powder, oregano, cumin, and salt. Tuck the red chile strips down into the mixture.

3. Cover and cook on the low heat setting about 8 hours. Serve with any or all of the garnishes.

Turkey and Black-Eyed Pea Chili

As this recipe demonstrates, you can make chili with many different kinds of beans. Use leftover cooked turkey or chicken breast in this variation and zip it up as much as desired with cayenne. Dried black-eyed peas cook more quickly in the slow cooker than other dry beans. This makes a great base for a tostada salad topped with lettuce, cheese, tomatoes, guacamole, and sour cream.

MAKES 5 TO 6 SERVINGS

1 (16-ounce) package dried black-eyed peas, rinsed, drained, and picked over
3 cups very hot water
5 teaspoons chili powder
2 teaspoons cumin seeds
2 garlic cloves, minced
Pinch of cayenne, or more to taste
2 medium onions, chopped
1 medium fresh poblano pepper, seeds and membranes removed, chopped, or ½ green bell pepper and ½ red bell pepper, chopped

1½ to 2 cups chopped cooked turkey or chicken breast
2 tablespoons tomato paste
1 cup prepared salsa
Chopped scallions, chopped tomatoes, shredded Cheddar cheese, and sour cream, for serving

1. In a 3½-quart electric slow cooker, mix together the black-eyed peas, hot water, 4 teaspoons of the chili powder, the cumin seeds, garlic, cayenne, onions, poblano pepper, and turkey.

2. Cover and cook on the high heat setting 1 hour. Reduce the heat setting to low and continue cooking, covered, 3 hours longer, or until the beans are tender but not mushy.

3. Stir in the remaining 1 teaspoon chili powder, the tomato paste, and the salsa. Serve topped with scallions, tomatoes, cheese, and a dollop of sour cream.

White Bean Turkey Chili

For best-tasting results, use ground turkey breast, which is available prepackaged in most supermarkets, for this chili.

1 pound ground turkey breast
2 tablespoons plus 2 teaspoons chili
   powder
1 tablespoon ground cumin
1 teaspoon sweet Hungarian paprika
½ teaspoon garlic powder
½ teaspoon seasoned salt

¼ teaspoon freshly ground pepper
1 (7-ounce) can diced green chiles
1 (16-ounce) package dried small
   white beans, rinsed, drained, and
   picked over
4 cups very hot water
2 medium onions, chopped

1. Crumble the turkey into a large hot skillet. Cook over medium-high heat, stirring often, until the turkey is cooked through, 7 to 10 minutes. Drain off any liquid. Turn into a 4-quart electric slow cooker. Add the chili powder, cumin, paprika, garlic powder, seasoned salt, and pepper. Mix well. Stir in the green chiles, beans, water, and onions.

2. Cover and cook on the high heat setting 1 hour. Reduce the heat setting to low and continue cooking 8 to 9 hours, or until the beans are tender.

Chicken Stew Mexican Style

Serve with plenty of warm tortillas or corn bread.

2 pounds skinless, boneless chicken breasts, cut into 1½-inch pieces

4 medium russet potatoes (about 1½ pounds), peeled and shredded

1 (15-ounce) can mild salsa

1 (4-ounce) can diced green chiles

1 (1¼-ounce) package taco seasoning mix

1 (8-ounce) can tomato sauce

1 (16-ounce) package frozen stringless young green beans, thawed, drained, and cut into 1-inch lengths

1. In a 3½-quart electric slow cooker, mix together the chicken pieces and potatoes. In a medium bowl, stir together the salsa, chiles, and taco seasoning mix. Pour over the chicken and potatoes and mix well; level the top. Pour the tomato sauce over all, spreading evenly; do not mix in.

2. Cover and cook on the low heat setting 5½ to 6 hours, or until the chicken and potatoes are tender.

3. Mix gently. Increase the heat setting to high. Stir in the green beans and cook, uncovered, on high 15 to 20 minutes, or until the beans are crisp-tender. Serve immediately.

Fisherman's Stew

This is reminiscent of a West Coast–style cioppino or bouillabaisse. If using frozen fish, be sure to thaw it first before adding to the slow cooker.

MAKES 4 TO 5 SERVINGS

1 (28-ounce) can diced peeled
    tomatoes
1 (6-ounce) can tomato paste
1 cup water
¾ cup dry white wine
1 medium onion, chopped
1 medium green bell pepper, chopped
3 celery ribs, chopped
2 garlic cloves, crushed through a
    press
2 teaspoons dried basil
½ teaspoon dried thyme leaves
1 bay leaf

½ teaspoon salt
¼ teaspoon freshly ground pepper
Pinch of sugar
½ pound shelled and deveined
    medium shrimp
½ pound small scallops
¾ pound halibut steak, skinned,
    boned, and cut into ¾-inch chunks
1 (4-ounce) can or jar mushroom
    stems and pieces or sliced mush-
    rooms, rinsed and drained
3 tablespoons chopped fresh parsley, for
    garnish

1. In a 3½-quart electric slow cooker, mix together the tomatoes with their liquid, tomato paste, water, wine, onion, green pepper, celery, garlic, basil, thyme, bay leaf, salt, and pepper.

2. Cover and cook on the low heat setting 5½ to 6 hours. Remove and discard the bay leaf. Stir in the sugar.

3. Increase the heat setting to high. Stir in the shrimp, scallops, and halibut. Cover and cook on high about 20 to 30 minutes, until the shrimp turn pink and the scallops and halibut turn white. Stir in the mushrooms. Serve in soup bowls, garnished with the parsley.

Chapter Four
Chicken and Turkey

With chicken and turkey the light meats of choice for more and more Americans these days, it is nice to discover innovative and interesting ways to simmer and serve them from a slow cooker. As with conventional cooking technologies, poultry generally cooks more quickly than most other meats. In most cases, skinless, boneless chicken will take from 3½ to 4½ hours, depending on the nature of the other foods in the pot. Even in the slow cooker, chicken is not an overnight proposition, so plan accordingly.

The recipes here rely mostly on skinless, boneless breasts, chicken tenders, chicken breast fillets, skinless chicken thighs, and turkey breast strips and pieces, and for good reason. When other chicken parts are used, even if they have been skinned (which can be tedious and time-consuming), you end up with what I consider undesirable amounts of fat in the finished dish. If that doesn't bother you or you don't agree, by all means go ahead and substitute your favorite parts for chicken breasts in the recipes. However, be aware that it may be necessary to increase or adjust cooking times accordingly. Even when using chicken breasts or chicken tenders in recipes, be sure to trim off all the visible fat before you add them to the pot.

And when using ground turkey or chicken, be sure to brown it as the recipes call for before adding to the slow cooker. This extra step is worth it to add appetizing color and to prevent the ground poultry from cooking in clumps.

Directions are also included for roasting a whole chicken in the slow cooker. No liquid is added and no tending is required. This effortless preparation can be a boon to hurried cooks who need tender, succulent, boneless chicken to use in casseroles, salads, and other dishes. If not using the chicken immediately, keep it refrigerated.

Chicken and poultry team well with a myriad of foods, including rice, potatoes, fruits, tomatoes, beans, and other vegetables. For a dinner party, offer Chicken with Potatoes, Sun-Dried Tomatoes, and Artichokes. Children adore the Barbecued Turkey Sloppy Joes. Fiesta Chicken and Potatoes utilizes packaged dried potatoes, which cook more quickly than fresh potatoes. Chicken is also cooked with frozen hash browns for a great hash-style dish. On the classic theme, you'll find dishes like Country Captain, Sweet-and-Sour Turkey and Vegetables, and Turkey Fajita Style. For those who like chicken thighs, try our version in orange sauce that uses skinless, boneless thighs.

Saucy Apricot-Glazed Chicken

This is a slow-cooker rendition of the ever-popular chicken glazed with a mixture of apricot preserves, Russian dressing, and dry onion soup mix that's usually baked in the oven. Cooked in the slow cooker, you end up with a lot of delicious, apricot-colored sauce to gussy up the chicken breasts. Serve over wild rice or white rice; or try basmati or jasmine rice, cooked on top of the stove. If you have leftover chicken and sauce, freeze and use within two months.

MAKES 8 TO 10 SERVINGS

1 cup good-quality chunky apricot
   preserves
¾ cup bottled Russian dressing
1 (1.15-ounce) envelope dry onion soup
   mix

12 skinless, boneless chicken breast
   halves, trimmed of fat (about 3½
   to 4 pounds)

1. In a medium bowl, mix together the apricot preserves, dressing, and dry soup mix until well blended. Arrange 3 of the chicken breast halves in the bottom of a 3½-quart electric slow cooker. Spoon a fourth of the apricot mixture on top. Add 3 more layers of chicken with the apricot mixture in between and on top.

2. Cover and cook on the high heat setting 1 hour. Reduce the heat setting to low and continue cooking, covered, 2½ to 3 hours, or until the chicken is tender and white throughout; do not overcook or the chicken will toughen. Serve the sauce over the chicken.

Chicken and Corn Hash

Using frozen hash browns to make this delicious potato dish speeds preparation time. If red bell pepper isn't available, substitute ½ cup roasted red pepper strips.

MAKES 6 SERVINGS

6 cups frozen hash brown potatoes (about 1½ pounds), partially thawed

1 large onion, chopped

1 (15¼-ounce) can whole kernel corn, drained

1 red bell pepper, chopped

1 (4-ounce) can diced green chiles

1 (4-ounce) can mushroom stems and pieces, drained

¼ teaspoon salt

¼ teaspoon freshly ground pepper

1 (10¾-ounce) can condensed cream of chicken soup (reduced-sodium, reduced-fat, if you have it)

½ cup water

½ cup dry white wine

1 pound skinless, boneless chicken breast fillets, cut into 1-inch cubes

Chopped fresh parsley or watercress, for garnish

1. In a 4-quart electric slow cooker, combine the potatoes, onion, corn, bell pepper, chiles, mushrooms, salt, and pepper. Mix well. In a medium bowl, stir together the undiluted soup with the water and wine until smooth. Stir into the potato mixture along with the chicken.

2. Cover and cook on the low heat setting 4½ to 5 hours, or until the chicken and potatoes are cooked through. Before serving, garnish the top with parsley or watercress.

Country Captain

Stories have it that a spice trade captain brought this curried chicken dish to America. I've added rice to turn it into a one-pot meal. For a festive touch, serve sprinkled with toasted almonds, coconut, and chopped scallions.

MAKES 5 TO 6 SERVINGS

1 (28-ounce) can diced peeled
   tomatoes
1 (15-ounce) can tomato sauce
1 medium onion, chopped
1 tart green apple, chopped
1 green bell pepper, chopped
⅓ cup raisins
1½ tablespoons Madras curry powder

¾ teaspoon garlic powder
½ teaspoon ground ginger
⅛ teaspoon cayenne
1½ cups converted white rice
6 skinless, boneless chicken breast
   halves, trimmed of fat (about 1½
   pounds)

1. In a 5-quart electric slow cooker, mix together the tomatoes with their liquid, tomato sauce, onion, apple, green pepper, raisins, curry powder, garlic powder, ginger, cayenne, and rice. Cut each chicken breast half crosswise into 5 pieces. Stir the chicken pieces into the mixture in the slow cooker.

2. Cover and cook on the low heat setting about 3½ hours, or until the chicken is cooked through and the rice is tender; do not overcook or the rice will be mushy.

Curried Chicken, Ham, and Rice

Much of the fun of eating a curry is choosing which condiments to add. Pass peanuts, sliced scallions, mango chutney, raisins, and shredded coconut, and let diners help themselves.

MAKES 6 TO 8 SERVINGS

1½ cups converted white rice
3½ cups boiling water
1 onion, quartered and thinly sliced
2½ teaspoons Madras curry powder
1 teaspoon ground cumin
¼ teaspoon turmeric
⅛ teaspoon cayenne

¼ teaspoon salt
¼ teaspoon garlic powder
1 pound chicken breast tenders, cut
   into thin strips
1 cup chopped cooked ham
1½ cups frozen peas, partially thawed

1. In a 4- or 5-quart electric slow cooker, mix together all the ingredients except the ham and peas.

2. Cover and cook on the high heat setting 1 hour. Reduce the heat setting to low and cook, covered, 2½ to 3 hours longer, or until the rice is tender but not mushy and the chicken is cooked through. Stir in the ham and peas; cover and let stand 10 minutes to heat through.

Chicken Deli Casserole

Here the flavors you'd find in a Reuben sandwich minus the bread are layered over low-fat skinless chicken instead of corned beef, for a family Sunday supper or Superbowl spread that's a snap to throw together. Serve slices of chewy rye or pumpernickel bread on the side; or ladle the casserole right onto the bread.

MAKES 4 TO 5 SERVINGS

1 (32-ounce) jar sauerkraut, rinsed and well drained
1 cup Russian dressing
6 skinless, boneless chicken breast halves, trimmed of fat

1 tablespoon prepared yellow mustard
1 cup shredded Swiss cheese
Fresh parsley, for garnish

1. Place half of the sauerkraut in a 3½-quart electric slow cooker. Drizzle on about ⅓ cup of the dressing. Top with 3 chicken breast halves and spread the mustard over the chicken. Top with the remaining sauerkraut and chicken breasts. Drizzle another ⅓ cup dressing over the casserole. Refrigerate the remaining dressing until serving time.

2. Cover and cook on the low heat setting about 3½ to 4 hours, or until the chicken is white throughout and tender.

3. To serve, spoon the casserole onto 4 or 5 plates. Sprinkle 3 to 4 tablespoons of cheese over and drizzle about 1 tablespoon of the Russian dressing on top. Serve immediately, garnished with parsley.

Easy Chicken Santa Fe

I like to serve this soupy chicken stew topped with chopped scallions and tomatoes, with a basket of warm tortillas on the side.

MAKES 5 TO 6 SERVINGS

1 (15-ounce) can black beans, rinsed and drained

2 (15¼-ounce) cans whole kernel corn, drained

1 cup bottled thick and chunky salsa

5 or 6 skinless, boneless chicken breast halves (about 2 pounds total), trimmed of all fat

1 cup shredded Cheddar cheese

1. In a 3½- or 4-quart electric slow cooker, mix together the beans, corn, and ½ cup salsa. Top with the chicken breasts, then pour the remaining ½ cup salsa over the chicken.

2. Cover and cook on the high heat setting 2½ to 3 hours, or until the chicken is tender and white throughout; do not overcook or the chicken will toughen.

3. Sprinkle the cheese on top, cover, and cook until the cheese melts, about 5 minutes.

Fiesta Chicken and Potatoes

If you love to entertain family and friends but don't have much time to spend in the kitchen, let your slow cooker and an array of fine convenience products assist in making this delicious dish. It's a winner.

MAKES 4 TO 6 SERVINGS

2 (11-ounce) cans fiesta nacho cheese soup
1 cup water
2 (5-ounce) packages dried homestyle skin-on potatoes with broccoli au gratin
6 scallions, thinly sliced
1 red bell pepper, diced
1 carrot, peeled and shredded
1 (7-ounce) can diced green chiles
2 pounds skinless, boneless chicken breast tenders

1. Mix the undiluted soup with the water and the sauce packets from the potato packages until well blended. Set aside.

2. Scatter the potatoes from 1 package over the bottom of a 4-quart electric slow cooker. Sprinkle with half of the scallions, bell pepper, carrot, and chiles. Place half of the chicken tenders on top and pour half of the sauce mixture over all. Repeat the layers with the remaining ingredients, ending with the rest of the sauce.

3. Cover and cook on the low heat setting about 4½ hours, or until the chicken is cooked through and the potatoes are tender.

Chicken with Figs and Lemon

This dish is exotic and unique with Moroccan flavors. The figs add a touch of sweetness and an interesting texture. Serve with couscous.

MAKES 6 TO 8 SERVINGS

1 (14½-ounce) can chicken broth
2 (1.7-ounce) boxes chicken Dijonne recipe mix, such as Knorr
1 teaspoon ground cinnamon
6 garlic cloves, minced

Grated zest and juice of 1 lemon
1 onion, quartered and thinly sliced
8 ounces dried Mission figs, halved
2 pounds skinless, boneless chicken breasts and thighs

1. In a 4-quart electric slow cooker, mix together the chicken broth, recipe mix, cinnamon, garlic, and zest and juice of the lemon. Stir in the onion and figs. Push the chicken pieces down into the mixture in the pot.

2. Cover and cook on the low heat setting about 4½ hours, or until the chicken is cooked through and tender but still moist.

Normandy Chicken with Apples

The flavor of the apples really comes through in this cold-weather dish. Complete the meal with a tossed green salad.

MAKES 6 TO 8 SERVINGS

3 cups apple cider

3 (1.8-ounce) boxes leek soup mix

2 teaspoons dried thyme leaves

½ teaspoon grated nutmeg

1½ pounds red potatoes, peeled and diced

4 celery ribs, thinly sliced

6 shallots, thinly sliced

3 green apples, cored and cut into 16 wedges each

¾ cup dried cranberries

2 pounds skinless, boneless chicken breast halves, halved crosswise

1. In a 4- or 5-quart electric slow cooker, combine the apple cider, dry soup mix, thyme, and nutmeg. Stir to blend well. Add the potatoes, celery, shallots, apples, and cranberries. Tuck the chicken pieces down into the mixture.

2. Cover and cook on the low heat setting about 8 hours, or until the potatoes are tender.

Chicken with Potatoes, Sun-Dried Tomatoes, and Artichokes

For a truly Mediterranean touch, crumble a little goat cheese or feta cheese over the top of this dish when serving.

MAKES 4 TO 5 SERVINGS

1¾ pounds small red potatoes, scrubbed and thinly sliced

¾ cup sun-dried tomatoes (do not rehydrate), coarsely cut up

¼ teaspoon garlic pepper

5 tablespoons balsamic vinegar

6 skinless, boneless chicken breast fillets or halves

½ cup roasted red pepper strips

1 (13¾-ounce) can quartered artichoke hearts, rinsed and well drained

3 tablespoons drained capers

¼ cup chopped fresh basil

1. Place the potatoes in a 3½- or 4-quart electric slow cooker. Sprinkle ½ cup of the sun-dried tomatoes and the garlic pepper over the potatoes. Drizzle on 3 tablespoons of the balsamic vinegar.

2. Cover and cook on the high heat setting 2 hours. Reduce the heat setting to low.

3. Place the chicken breasts on top of the potatoes. Sprinkle the remaining ¼ cup sun-dried tomatoes, the roasted pepper strips, and the artichoke hearts over the chicken. Cover and cook on low about 3 hours, or until the potatoes are tender and the chicken is cooked through. Drizzle the remaining 2 tablespoons vinegar over the top and garnish with the capers and basil.

Quick-Fix Layered Chicken Casserole

No chopping is required here; this recipe relies on a package of scalloped potatoes, frozen vegetables, canned soup, and chicken tenders. If you don't tell, no one will guess your shortcuts.

MAKES 4 SERVINGS

1 (5-ounce) package scalloped potatoes
1 (10¾-ounce) can condensed cream of mushroom soup
1 cup water
½ teaspoon garlic pepper
1 (16-ounce) package frozen mixed vegetables (broccoli, carrots, and cauliflower), thawed and drained

1 (16-ounce) package frozen stir-fry vegetables (broccoli, sugar snap peas, green beans, carrots, celery, water chestnuts, onions, and peppers), thawed and drained
1 pound skinless, boneless chicken breast tenders
Paprika

1. Place the dried potatoes from the package in a 3½-quart electric slow cooker. In a medium bowl, mix the undiluted soup with the water, the sauce packet from the potato package, and the garlic pepper until well blended. Drizzle just a little of this soup mixture over the potatoes. Then layer the remaining ingredients in the slow cooker as follows: the package of mixed vegetables plus ⅓ of the stir-fry vegetables, ⅔ of the chicken tenders, ⅔ of the remaining soup mixture, remaining stir-fry vegetables, and remaining chicken tenders. Pour the remaining soup mixture evenly over the chicken.

2. Cover and cook on the low heat setting about 4½ hours, or until the chicken and potatoes are tender and cooked through. Sprinkle paprika over the top. Serve at once.

Slow-Cooker Roasted Chicken

A slow cooker is a great way to cook a whole chicken to tender perfection. No liquid is added to the cooker, and no tending is required—a boon to busy cooks. For best results, remove as much skin and fat from the chicken as possible prior to cooking. Although the chicken won't be browned, I've added a spice rub for some color.

MAKES 4 SERVINGS

1 (4-pound) chicken
1 teaspoon paprika
½ teaspoon dried thyme leaves
½ teaspoon dried basil
½ teaspoon Beau Monde seasoning

½ teaspoon seasoned salt
½ teaspoon garlic powder
½ teaspoon freshly ground pepper
1 tablespoon olive oil

1. Remove the giblets from the chicken. Remove as much fat and skin as possible. Rinse and drain the chicken; pat dry inside and out with paper towels. Mix all the seasonings with the olive oil to make a paste. Spread a little of the seasoning paste inside the cavity. Place the chicken, breast side up, in a 3½- or 4-quart electric slow cooker. Spread the remaining seasoning over the top of the chicken.
2. Cover and cook on the high heat setting 3 to 3½ hours (6½ to 7½ hours on low), or until the chicken is cooked through and the juices run clear. Cut into pieces and serve immediately. Or cool slightly, remove the chicken from the bones, and use in pastas, salads, or casseroles. If not using the boned chicken immediately, refrigerate and use within a day or two. Reserve the juices in the bottom of the slow cooker, if desired; chill and remove the fat, then use in making soup, sauces, etc.

Spanish Chicken with Olives

Garbanzo beans, otherwise known as chick-peas, and pimiento-stuffed olives add interest to this zesty casserole.

MAKES 4 SERVINGS

1 (15½-ounce) can garbanzo beans (chick-peas), rinsed and drained
1 cup converted white rice
1 onion, quartered and thinly sliced
1 green bell pepper, cut into ¼-inch-wide strips
1 (14½-ounce) can diced peeled tomatoes
½ cup water
½ teaspoon garlic powder

Pinch of saffron threads
⅔ cup coarsely chopped pimiento-stuffed olives
4 skinless, boneless chicken breast halves, trimmed of fat (about 1¼ pounds)
½ teaspoon paprika
½ teaspoon garlic pepper
2 tablespoons chopped fresh parsley

1. In a 3½- or 4-quart electric slow cooker, mix together the garbanzo beans, rice, onion, bell pepper, tomatoes with their liquid, water, garlic powder, saffron, and ⅓ cup of the olives. Top with the chicken. Season with the paprika and garlic pepper.
2. Cover and cook on the low heat setting about 4 hours, or until the chicken is cooked through and the rice is tender; do not overcook or the rice will be mushy.
3. Mix in the remaining ⅓ cup olives. Serve garnished with the parsley.

Tex-Mex Chicken 'N' Rice

This is a great dish to take to a potluck party. It goes together in a jiffy with a package of taco seasoning mix.

2 cups converted white rice
1 (28-ounce) can diced peeled
  tomatoes
1 (6-ounce) can tomato paste
3 cups hot water
1 (1.04-ounce) package chicken taco
  seasoning mix

4 skinless, boneless chicken breast
  halves, cut into ½-inch cubes
2 medium onions, chopped
1 green bell pepper, chopped
1 (4-ounce) can diced green chiles
¾ teaspoon garlic pepper

1. In a 5-quart electric slow cooker, mix together all the ingredients except the chiles and garlic pepper.

2. Cover and cook on the low heat setting 4 to 4½ hours, or until the rice is tender and the chicken is white throughout; do not overcook or the rice will be mushy.

3. Stir in the green chiles and garlic pepper and serve at once.

Chicken Thighs in Orange-Tomato Sauce

To avoid ending up with a fatty sauce, purchase skinless, boneless chicken thighs to use in this dish. Serve over hot steamed rice, mashed potatoes, or polenta.

MAKES 5 TO 6 SERVINGS

2 pounds skinless, boneless chicken
thighs, trimmed of fat and cut into
1- to 1½-inch pieces
1 (14½-ounce) can diced peeled
tomatoes
Grated zest of 2 large oranges
Juice of 1 large orange
1 (6-ounce) can tomato paste
1 medium onion, chopped
2 cups diced carrots (3 or 4)
1 tablespoon dried basil

1 teaspoon dried oregano
½ teaspoon dried thyme leaves,
crushed
½ teaspoon dried rosemary, crumbled
2 garlic cloves, crushed through a
press
½ teaspoon freshly ground pepper
1½ teaspoons sugar
2 tablespoons lemon juice
4 slices of lean bacon, cooked until
crisp and crumbled

1. In a 3½-quart electric slow cooker, combine the chicken pieces, tomatoes with their liquid, zest of 1 orange, orange juice, tomato paste, onion, carrots, basil, oregano, thyme, rosemary, garlic, and pepper; mix well.

2. Cover and cook on the low heat setting 6 to 6½ hours, or until the chicken is cooked through. Stir in the sugar, lemon juice, and zest of the remaining orange. Sprinkle the top of each serving with a little crumbled bacon.

Tamale Casserole

This is a great dish to share with friends on a cold day. It is easily assembled with store-bought tamales and needs no attention all day. Served with a salad, it's a complete meal. And you can be sure everyone will come back for more.

1 large onion, diced

1 (16-ounce) jar green tomatillo salsa

2 (15-ounce) cans chili con carne without beans

1 (15-ounce) can black beans, rinsed and drained

1 (2¼-ounce) can sliced ripe olives, drained

8 to 10 chicken or beef tamales, wrappers or husks removed

2 (7-ounce) cans whole green chiles, drained and cut into ½-inch strips

Shredded Cheddar cheese and sour cream, as accompaniments

1. Place half of the diced onions in a 4-quart electric slow cooker. Top with half each of the salsa, the chili, beans, and olives. Place 4 or 5 of the tamales on top. Cover the tamales with half of the chile strips. Repeat the layers, ending with the remaining chile strips.

2. Cover and cook on the low heat setting 6½ to 7 hours. Pass shredded cheese and sour cream on the side.

Barbecued Turkey Sloppy Joes

Serve on toasted split sourdough rolls or in small individual hollowed-out round bread loaves or rolls.

MAKES 8 SERVINGS

2 pounds ground turkey
2 medium onions, chopped
2 (15-ounce) cans tomato sauce
1 (6-ounce) can tomato paste
½ cup packed brown sugar
⅓ cup red wine vinegar
2 tablespoons Worcestershire sauce
2 tablespoons liquid smoke hickory
    flavoring

½ teaspoon seasoned salt
¼ teaspoon freshly ground pepper
8 sourdough rolls, split and toasted, or
    toasted bread slices or small individ-
    ual round bread loaves, tops cut off
    and hollowed out (pull out some of
    bread inside)

1. In a large skillet or flameproof casserole on top of the stove, cook the turkey and onions over medium-high heat, stirring often, until the turkey is lightly browned and crumbly, 6 to 8 minutes. Drain off excess liquid.

2. Transfer the turkey mixture to a 3½- or 4-quart electric slow cooker. Stir in the tomato sauce, tomato paste, brown sugar, vinegar, Worcestershire sauce, 5 teaspoons of the liquid smoke, the seasoned salt, and pepper.

3. Cover and cook on the low heat setting 6 to 7 hours. Stir in the remaining 1 teaspoon liquid smoke. Serve on sourdough roll halves, on bread slices, or in small bread loaves.

Turkey Fajita Style

While this appealing stew has many of the same ingredients as fajitas, don't expect it to taste exactly the same as when the turkey is grilled. Accompany with warm flour tortillas, chopped tomatoes, guacamole or diced avocado, and sour cream.

MAKES 4 SERVINGS

2 green bell peppers, cut into thin strips
1 red bell pepper, cut into thin strips
1 yellow bell pepper, cut into thin strips
2 medium onions, halved and cut into thin wedges
1 to 1½ pounds skinless, boneless turkey breast strips

2 teaspoons ground cumin
2 teaspoons chili powder
½ teaspoon garlic powder
½ teaspoon paprika
¼ teaspoon freshly ground black pepper
⅛ teaspoon cayenne
¼ cup plus 2 tablespoons fresh lime juice

1. In a 3½-quart electric slow cooker, combine all the bell peppers with the onions. In a small bowl, mix together the turkey strips, cumin, chili powder, garlic powder, paprika, black pepper, cayenne, and ¼ cup lime juice. Turn into the slow cooker over the vegetable mixture.

2. Cover and cook on the low heat setting 2 hours. Stir and cook, covered, 1 to 1½ hours longer, or until the turkey is cooked through. Just before serving, stir in the remaining 2 tablespoons lime juice.

Turkey Mexicali

This colorful mélange is great to roll up in warm flour tortillas along with shredded cheese and sour cream. Chicken strips can be used instead of turkey, if you prefer. The mixture also makes a tasty base for tostada salads.

MAKES 4 SERVINGS

1 pound skinless, boneless turkey breast strips or skinless, boneless chicken breasts, cut into thin strips

1 (15¼-ounce) can whole kernel corn, drained

1 (15-ounce) can black beans, rinsed and well drained

1 tablespoon ground cumin

1 teaspoon chili powder

1 onion, halved and cut into thin wedges

1 green bell pepper, cut into thin strips 1½ inches long

1 (14½-ounce) can diced peeled tomatoes, undrained

1 (6-ounce) can tomato paste

1. In a 3½-quart electric slow cooker, combine all the ingredients; mix well.

2. Cover and cook on the low heat setting 4½ to 5 hours, or until the turkey is cooked through.

Turkey Breast with Pineapple, Tomatoes, and Peppers

This dish has classic flavor and is a cinch to prepare in the slow cooker. Serve with hot steamed rice.

MAKES 5 TO 6 SERVINGS

1 (20-ounce) can unsweetened
   pineapple chunks
1 large green bell pepper, cut into
   1-inch squares
1 medium red bell pepper, cut into
   1-inch squares
1 large onion, cut into wedges
¼ cup ketchup
3 tablespoons red wine vinegar

3 tablespoons brown sugar
1 (2-pound) skinless, boneless turkey
   breast
¼ teaspoon seasoned salt
1½ tablespoons cornstarch
2 (10-ounce) packages frozen Chinese
   snow peas, thawed and drained
2 large tomatoes, cut into wedges

1. Drain the pineapple chunks, reserving 3 tablespoons juice. In a 3½- or 4-quart electric slow cooker, combine half of the drained pineapple chunks with the green and red peppers, onion, and 2 tablespoons each of the ketchup, vinegar, and brown sugar. Mix well. Add the turkey breast; sprinkle with seasoned salt. Top with the remaining pineapple chunks.

2. Cover and cook on the high heat setting 3½ to 4 hours, or until the turkey is cooked through, tender and white in the center. Remove the turkey breast.

3. Stir in the remaining 2 tablespoons ketchup, 1 tablespoon vinegar, and 1 tablespoon brown sugar. Dissolve the cornstarch in the reserved 3 tablespoons pineapple juice and stir into the sauce. Cover and cook on high 20 to 30 minutes longer, or until thickened slightly, stirring once.

4. Stir in the snow peas and tomato wedges and heat 5 minutes longer. Carve the turkey breast into slices before serving.

Sweet-and-Sour Turkey and Vegetables

Buy prepackaged cut-up turkey breast strips available in most supermarkets and frozen vegetable mixtures to speed up the preparation of this Chinese-inspired, sweet-and-sour meal in a dish. Check as it nears the end of the suggested cooking time to avoid overcooking the rice and vegetables. Top each serving with a sprinkling of peanuts or cashews.

MAKES 4 TO 5 SERVINGS

1 (16-ounce) package frozen stir-fry vegetables with rice, partially thawed

1 (16-ounce) package frozen stir-fry vegetables, partially thawed

½ cup prepared Chinese sweet-and-sour sauce

3 tablespoons white or red wine vinegar

3 tablespoons hoisin sauce

1½ teaspoons Chinese chili paste with garlic

1 pound skinless, boneless turkey breast strips

1 (10-ounce) package frozen pea pods, thawed and drained (optional)

½ teaspoon salt

½ teaspoon freshly ground pepper

1. In a 3½- or 4-quart electric slow cooker, combine both types of stir-fry vegetables. In a small bowl, mix together the sweet-and-sour sauce, 2 tablespoons each of the vinegar and hoisin sauce, and the chili paste with garlic. Add half of this sauce to the vegetable mixture and mix well. Stir in the turkey strips and the remaining sauce, mixing well.

2. Cover and cook on the low heat setting 4 to 4½ hours, or until the turkey is cooked through, stirring once during the cooking time, if possible.

3. Stir in the remaining 1 tablespoon vinegar and hoisin sauce along with the pea pods, salt, and pepper. Let stand 5 minutes before serving.

Chapter Five
Meaty Mainstays

With the slow cooker, you can turn out old-fashioned, succulent meat dishes with a minimum of effort and attention. Even better, these dishes are often economical because they utilize inexpensive cuts of beef, lamb, veal, and pork, which are tenderized during long, slow cooking. Most of these recipes are remarkably quick to assemble, and then you're on your way to work or to a day away from the kitchen.

They generally call for cut-up beef round steak or boneless beef chuck, ground beef, ham, beef shanks, lamb shanks, lamb stew meat, sausages, or ribs. A few opt for larger pieces of meat, such as pot roast, chuck or rump roast, beef brisket, corned beef brisket, veal shoulder, or round bone roast. Purchase these cuts with an eye to fitting them into the size and shape pot you're planning to cook them in. You may find it necessary to trim a large roast into two or three pieces to fit into the pot.

Keep in mind that ground beef is one exception, where the best-eating result is achieved by browning the meat before adding it to the slow cooker. If you don't, it ends up mealy and gray. However, it's not necessary to prebrown or precook any of the other meats.

The most important consideration when cooking meats in the slow cooker is to use cuts that are lean and trimmed of as much visible fat as possible. If you're cutting up the meat yourself, be sure to trim off all the fat you can as you cut the meat into smaller pieces. Even if you purchase meat that is already cut up, go over it yourself one more time to be sure it is as lean as possible. If you don't, you'll end up with excess grease floating on top of the finished dish. Of course, much of it can be skimmed off, but that is often a time-consuming chore. It's easier to avoid the problem in the first place.

You may notice that only small amounts of liquid are added to many of these dishes at the outset. That's because liquid will accumulate from the meats and other ingredients as well as from the moisture that condenses inside the slow cooker. Often times, more liquid is produced than desired. In these recipes, I thicken the dishes by stirring in a little dissolved cornstarch or quick-mixing flour near the end and then cooking on high about 20 to 30 minutes. If there's too much liquid, feel free to drain some of it off. And if you're in a rush, you can thicken the gravy or sauce more quickly on top of the stove by adding the cornstarch or flour mixture, bringing it to a boil, and boiling 1 to 2 minutes. The choice is yours.

Remember if you have any leftovers to refrigerate them promptly after cooking. Most of these dishes are good reheated, or they can be frozen to use at a later date.

One last note—this chapter ends with two shrimp recipes. Since I don't favor fish in the slow cooker, but did want to include at least a couple of seafood recipes, this seemed like the best place to tuck them in. Both are one-pot meals, and each is outstanding.

Barbecue Beef Brisket

Here's a simple and great-tasting way to prepare brisket that's easy on the cook. Serve with mashed potatoes and green beans. Or, to soak up the sauce, make barbecued beef sandwiches by serving over split, toasted sourdough or French rolls or toasted sourdough bread slices.

MAKES 6 SERVINGS

1 (2-pound) boneless beef brisket, trimmed of fat

2 cups prepared hickory-flavored barbecue sauce

1. Place the brisket in a 3½-quart electric slow cooker. Top with 1 cup barbecue sauce.

2. Cover and cook on the high setting 4 to 5 hours, or until the beef is tender. Stir in the remaining 1 cup barbecue sauce. Cover and cook 15 to 30 minutes longer, or until heated through.

3. Remove the brisket and skim off any fat from the sauce. Slice the meat across the grain and serve topped with the sauce.

Ranch-Style Brisket and Beans

Whether you're serving indoors or out, this is a great one-dish barbecue. Accompany with coleslaw and corn bread for a complete Western feast.

MAKES 6 TO 8 SERVINGS

1 (16-ounce) package dried pinto
    beans, rinsed, drained, and picked
    over
2 cups hot water
1 large onion, chopped
1½ cups ketchup
3 tablespoons Worcestershire sauce
1 tablespoon prepared yellow mustard

¼ cup red wine vinegar
¼ cup packed brown sugar
½ teaspoon seasoned salt
1 teaspoon liquid smoke hickory
    flavoring
1 (3-pound) boneless beef brisket,
    trimmed of fat

1. In a 4- or 5-quart electric slow cooker, combine the pinto beans, water, and onion. In a medium bowl, mix together the ketchup, Worcestershire sauce, mustard, vinegar, brown sugar, seasoned salt, and liquid smoke. Stir half of the ketchup mixture into the beans in the slow cooker. Place the brisket on top of the beans; cut to fit into the pot if necessary. Spread the remaining ketchup mixture over the top of the brisket.

2. Cover and cook on the low heat setting 9 to 10 hours, stirring once or twice, if possible, until the beans and beef are tender. Skim off any excess fat from the top. To serve, slice the meat across the grain and serve with the beans.

Beef and Beans South of the Border

This versatile mixture is excellent fare for serving a casual crowd. It makes a good filling for burritos, tacos, enchiladas, and tostadas, and is especially convenient for last-minute suppers because it freezes well, too. I like to roll it up in warm flour tortillas with shredded Cheddar cheese, chopped scallions, salsa, sour cream, and guacamole.

MAKES 8 TO 10 SERVINGS

1 (16-ounce) package dried small white beans or 1¼ cups dried small white beans and 1¼ cups dried small red beans, rinsed, drained, and picked over
4 cups very hot water
1 (28-ounce) can diced peeled tomatoes
1 (7-ounce) can diced green chiles
4 garlic cloves, crushed through a press
2 tablespoons ground cumin

2 tablespoons chili powder
4 teaspoons dried oregano
1 teaspoon ground coriander
1 teaspoon salt
¼ teaspoon freshly ground black pepper
¼ teaspoon cayenne
1½ to 2 pounds boneless beef top sirloin steak or boneless beef top round steak, trimmed of fat and cut into ½-inch cubes

1. In a 5- or 6-quart electric slow cooker, mix together the beans, hot water, tomatoes with their liquid, green chiles, garlic, cumin, chili powder, oregano, coriander, salt, black pepper, cayenne, and beef.

2. Cover and cook on the high heat setting 1 hour. Reduce the heat to the low setting and cook, covered, 8 hours longer, or until the beans and beef are tender. Season with additional salt and pepper to taste.

Beef Stroganoff

This is the hassle-free, no-tending way to make the delicious classic dish. Serve over noodles or rice and top with a sprinkling of chopped parsley for color.

MAKES 6 SERVINGS

2 pounds beef top round steak, trimmed of fat
½ pound fresh white mushrooms, sliced
1 bunch of scallions, chopped
1 medium onion, sliced
¼ teaspoon dried thyme leaves
¾ cup dry sherry

¾ cup homemade or canned beef broth
¾ teaspoon dry mustard
¼ teaspoon garlic pepper
1½ cups sour cream
½ cup quick-mixing flour, such as Wondra

1. Cut the beef into thin slices across the grain. Place in a 3½- or 4-quart electric slow cooker. Add the mushrooms, scallions, onion, thyme, sherry, broth, dry mustard, and garlic pepper. Mix well.

2. Cover and cook on the low heat setting about 8 hours, or until the beef is tender, stirring once, if possible. Increase the heat setting to high.

3. Mix together the sour cream and flour until thoroughly blended. Stir a little of the hot liquid from the slow cooker into the sour cream mixture; then stir the sour cream mixture into the slow cooker, mixing well. Cover and cook on high 30 to 40 minutes, or until thickened slightly.

Island Beef

If you're looking for sweet-and-sour flavor in a slow cooker, try this dish with strips of beef, tangy pineapple, green peppers, and tomatoes in a sweet-and-sour–flavored brown sauce. Serve over steamed white rice.

2 to 2½ pounds beef top round steak, trimmed of fat

2 large onions, cut into 12 thin wedges each

1 (20-ounce) can unsweetened pineapple chunks, juice reserved

½ cup homemade or canned beef broth

5 tablespoons red wine vinegar

¾ teaspoon garlic powder

¾ teaspoon seasoned salt

¾ teaspoon imported sweet paprika

¼ teaspoon freshly ground black pepper

1 green bell pepper, cut into 1-inch squares

1 red bell pepper, cut into 1-inch squares

3 tablespoons brown sugar

1½ tablespoons cornstarch

2 tablespoons soy sauce

2 large tomatoes, cut into wedges

1. Cut the beef into thin strips diagonally across the grain. Add to a 3½- or 4-quart electric slow cooker. Add the onions, pineapple juice, broth, 3 tablespoons of the vinegar, the garlic powder, seasoned salt, paprika, and black pepper. Mix well.

2. Cover and cook on the low heat setting 6 to 6½ hours, or until the beef is just tender.

3. Increase the heat setting to high. Stir in the green and red pepper squares and the brown sugar. Mix together the cornstarch, soy sauce, and remaining 2 tablespoons vinegar. Stir into the cooker, blending well. Cook, covered, on high 45 to 60 minutes, stirring occasionally, until the sauce thickens slightly. Just before serving, stir in the tomato wedges and pineapple chunks.

Swiss Steak with Baby Onions

Swiss steak is an old family favorite that brings back fond memories to me. Serve this updated version with mashed potatoes to soak up all the savory sauce and zucchini.

MAKES 6 TO 8 SERVINGS

3 (1.1-ounce) packages Hunter Sauce
   Mix, such as Knorr
1 (11½-ounce) can vegetable juice
   cocktail, such as V8
1 tablespoon tomato paste
1 tablespoon Worcestershire sauce
1 (16-ounce) package frozen baby
   onions (do not thaw)
1 celery rib, thinly sliced
½ pound fresh white mushrooms,
   sliced
3 pounds beef top round steak, cut
   1 inch thick, trimmed of fat, and
   cut into 4-inch-square serving pieces

1. In a medium bowl, mix together the dry sauce mix, vegetable juice, tomato paste, and Worcestershire sauce until well blended. Set aside.

2. In a 3½- or 4-quart electric slow cooker, place ⅓ each of the baby onions, celery, and mushrooms. Top with half of the meat pieces and ⅓ of the sauce mixture. Repeat the layers, then top with the remaining ⅓ each of the vegetables and sauce mixture.

3. Cover and cook on the low heat setting 9 to 10 hours, or until the meat is tender.

Asian Pot Roast

A favorite recipe shared by a friend, this meat has Asian overtones. Serve the meat and sauce over hot steamed rice and accompany with plenty of colorful stir-fried vegetables.

MAKES 8 SERVINGS

1 (14½-ounce) can chicken broth
2 teaspoons minced fresh ginger
4 garlic cloves, peeled and halved
½ cup soy sauce
1 (2½- to 3-pound) lean boneless beef pot roast or beef top round steak, trimmed of fat and cut into 3 or 4 chunks

2 large onions, sliced and separated into rings
¼ cup quick-mixing flour, such as Wondra

1. In a 3½- or 4-quart electric slow cooker, mix together the chicken broth, ginger, garlic, and soy sauce. Place the beef chunks in the broth mixture. Top with the onion slices.

2. Cover and cook on the low heat setting 8 to 9 hours, or until the beef is tender. If necessary, skim off any fat from the juices. In a small bowl, whisk together the flour and ¾ cup liquid from the slow cooker until smooth. Stir the flour mixture back into the liquid in the slow cooker. Increase the heat to the high setting and cook, uncovered, on high 30 to 40 minutes longer, or until the sauce is thickened slightly. Cut the meat into slices before serving.

Hungarian Beef Goulash

This old-world–style dish is delicious with or without the caraway seeds. It's good served with red cabbage or a spinach salad and chewy rye bread.

MAKES 4 SERVINGS

2 medium onions, halved and sliced
1½ pounds boneless beef chuck or beef round steak, trimmed of fat and cut into 1-inch cubes
4 teaspoons imported sweet paprika
¼ teaspoon freshly ground pepper
3 tablespoons ketchup
2 tablespoons water

¾ pound small red potatoes, scrubbed and shredded
1 (14½-ounce) can sauerkraut, rinsed and well drained
½ cup sour cream
½ to 1 teaspoon caraway seeds (optional)
Chopped fresh parsley, for garnish

1. In a 3½-quart electric slow cooker, mix together the onions, beef, paprika, pepper, ketchup, water, and potatoes. Top with the sauerkraut.

2. Cover and cook on the low heat setting 8 hours, or until the beef is tender. Mix gently. Stir in the sour cream and caraway seeds. Serve garnished with chopped fresh parsley.

Smoky Beef and Black-Eyed Peas

Country cooking doesn't come any better. For a real down-home meal, serve with braised collards or kale and Cheddared biscuits.

MAKES 8 TO 10 SERVINGS

1 (16-ounce) package dried black-eyed peas, rinsed and picked over
1 (11½-ounce) can bean with bacon soup
3 cups hot water
3 medium carrots, chopped
2 medium onions, sliced
1 teaspoon garlic powder
½ teaspoon seasoned salt
1 (3-pound) beef chuck roast, trimmed of fat and cut into 2-inch chunks
1 teaspoon liquid smoke hickory flavoring
1 (4-ounce) can diced green chiles
1 red bell pepper, chopped

1. In a 5- or 6-quart electric slow cooker, mix together the beans, undiluted soup, hot water, carrots, onions, garlic powder, and seasoned salt. Place the roast on top; press into the bean mixture to cover as much as possible.

2. Cover and cook on the low heat setting 9 to 10 hours, or until the beef and beans are tender.

3. Increase the heat setting to high. Stir in the liquid smoke, chiles, and bell pepper. Cook, uncovered, on high 10 to 15 minutes longer. Skim any excess fat from the top before serving.

Mushroom-Sauced Beef

Serve this old-fashioned comfort food with hot cooked noodles and a big tossed green salad.

MAKES 5 TO 6 SERVINGS

½ pound fresh white mushrooms, sliced

1 medium onion, sliced

1 (10¾-ounce) can condensed cream of mushroom soup

⅓ cup dry red wine

2 tablespoons Worcestershire sauce

1 (4-ounce) can diced green chiles

1 (2½-pound) boneless beef chuck or cross rib roast, trimmed of fat

3 tablespoons quick-mixing flour, such as Wondra

1. In a 4-quart electric slow cooker, combine ⅔ of the mushrooms and the onion. In a small bowl, whisk together the undiluted soup with the wine, 1 tablespoon of the Worcestershire sauce, and the chiles. Pour half of the soup mixture over the mushrooms and onion in the slow cooker. Cut the beef horizontally into 2 pieces, each about ¾ inch thick. Place on top of the mushroom mixture. Scatter the remaining mushroom slices over the meat and pour the remaining soup mixture evenly over all. Do not mix.

2. Cover and cook on the low heat setting about 8 hours, or until the beef is tender but not falling apart. Increase the heat setting to high

3. Mix the remaining 1 tablespoon Worcestershire sauce with the flour and several spoonfuls of the liquid from the slow cooker until smooth. Stir the flour mixture into the sauce in the slow cooker. Cover and cook on high ½ hour, or until slightly thickened.

Lemony Beef Shanks

Beef shanks cook to toothsome tenderness in the slow cooker. Serve with a fresh fruit salad and dark bread to soak up all the flavorful sauce.

MAKES 5 TO 6 SERVINGS

1 (12-ounce) can beer
1 (6-ounce) can tomato paste
¼ cup quick-mixing flour, such as Wondra
¼ teaspoon salt
¼ teaspoon freshly ground pepper
4 garlic cloves, minced
1 medium onion, thinly sliced

½ pound fresh white mushrooms, sliced
3 carrots, peeled and sliced
1¼ pounds red potatoes, scrubbed and cut into 1-inch cubes
2½ to 2¾ pounds beef shanks (use boneless, if desired), trimmed of fat
1 tablespoon grated lemon zest
2 tablespoons lemon juice

1. In a 3½-quart electric slow cooker, mix together the beer and tomato paste. Whisk in the flour, salt, pepper, and garlic until well blended. Stir in the onion, mushrooms, carrots, and potatoes. Add the beef shanks and push down into the vegetable mixture.

2. Cover and cook on the low heat setting 8½ to 9 hours, or until the beef and potatoes are tender. Stir in the lemon zest and lemon juice just before serving.

Old-Fashioned Sunday Supper

Who doesn't remember grandmother's beautiful platter heaped with potatoes, vegetables, and meat—all covered with a rich brown gravy. With today's slow cookers, this one-dish meal is a cinch to make.

MAKES 6 TO 8 SERVINGS

1 (2.2-ounce) box beefy onion soup mix (2 envelopes)

1 (3½-pound) beef rump roast, trimmed of fat

2 pounds small red potatoes, scrubbed and halved

3 large carrots, peeled and sliced

2 celery ribs, sliced

7 garlic cloves, minced

½ teaspoon garlic pepper

2 teaspoons dried thyme leaves

1 bay leaf

1½ cups zinfandel or other fruity red wine

1 (14½-ounce) can beef broth

¼ cup all-purpose flour

1. Place the contents of both of the dry soup mix envelopes in a small baking dish. Place the roast in the dish and rub or pat the dry soup mix all over it.

2. In a 5-quart electric slow cooker, place half each of the potatoes, carrots, celery, and garlic. Season with half each of the garlic pepper and thyme. Tuck the bay leaf into the vegetables. Mix together 1 cup of the wine and the broth. Pour into the slow cooker. Add the roast and scrape any dry soup mix left in the baking dish on top. Cover the meat with the remaining vegetables, garlic, garlic pepper, and thyme.

3. Cover and cook on the low heat setting 9 to 10 hours, or until the meat is tender.

4. Remove the meat to a warm serving platter. Remove and discard the bay leaf. Scoop out the vegetables with a slotted spoon and scatter them over and around the roast. Cover with foil to keep warm. Pour the juices from the slow cooker into a medium saucepan and bring to a boil on top of the stove over medium-high heat. Whisk together the remaining ½ cup wine and the flour until well blended. Stir into the juices in the saucepan and cook, stirring constantly, until the gravy is thickened and the flour has lost its raw taste, 3 to 5 minutes. Pour the gravy over the meat and vegetables and serve.

Slow and Easy Sauerbraten

For convenience, good color, and flavor, use a packaged sauerbraten mix in this rendition of the classic. Ignore the package directions regarding the liquid amount and follow the directions below instead.

4 russet potatoes, peeled and cut into ¼-inch-thick slices (about 1¾ pounds)

4 cups shredded red or green cabbage

3 pounds beef chuck, rump, or round roast, trimmed of as much fat as possible

1 (2-ounce) package sauerbraten beef pot roast recipe mix

½ cup water

1 tablespoon red wine vinegar

1. Layer the potatoes in the bottom of a 4-quart electric slow cooker. Add the cabbage and top with the roast. Mix together the dry sauerbraten mix and water until well blended. Pour over the roast.

2. Cover and cook on the low heat setting 9 to 10 hours, or until the beef is tender. Skim off and discard any fat from the sauce. Gently stir in the vinegar. Cut the meat into pieces before serving.

San Pasqual Beef Shanks with Black Beans

This is named after the street on which the friend who shared it with me lives. The chipotle chiles lend a pleasant, slightly smoky flavor and although the dish is not too spicy, you can make it hotter by increasing the amount of chipotle chiles. For color, serve garnished with shredded radishes and chopped cilantro.

MAKES 6 SERVINGS

1 (16-ounce) package dried black beans, rinsed and picked over
1 large onion, chopped
1 (28-ounce) can cut-up peeled tomatoes
1 (7-ounce) can diced green chiles
7 garlic cloves, minced
1 (14½-ounce) can beef broth
1 tablespoon ground cumin

1 tablespoon dried oregano
1 teaspoon salt
1 tablespoon diced canned chipotle chiles in adobo sauce
3½ pounds beef shanks, trimmed of fat
¼ cup masa harina
Grated zest and juice of 1 lime
1 (15-ounce) can hominy, drained

1. In a 6-quart electric slow cooker, combine the dried beans, onion, tomatoes with their liquid, green chiles, garlic, broth, cumin, oregano, salt, and chipotle chiles. Mix well. Add the beef shanks and push them down into the bean mixture.
2. Cover and cook on the low heat setting 9 to 10 hours, or until the beef and beans are tender.
3. Remove the beef shanks to a cutting board. Skim off any excess fat from the top of the beans. Increase the heat to the high setting and sprinkle the masa harina over the beans; mix to blend well. Stir in the lime zest, lime juice, and hominy. Remove the bones from the beef shanks and return the meat to the slow cooker. Cover and cook 15 minutes longer, until heated through.

Chop Suey Ground Beef Supper

Add the vegetables to this American-style creation made with ground beef during the last part of the cooking time so they end up crisp-tender. Before serving, stir in another tablespoon of soy sauce for a more pronounced Asian flavor.

MAKES 4 TO 5 SERVINGS

1 pound lean ground beef
1 onion, chopped
1 (6-ounce) package long-grain and wild rice mix
1¾ cups water
5 tablespoons soy sauce
1 (12-ounce) package fresh cut-up chop suey vegetables or a mixture of 2 cups shredded cabbage, 1 cup bean sprouts, 1 cup thin strips of carrots, and 1 cup thin strips of celery
½ pound fresh white mushrooms, sliced

1. In a large skillet on top of the stove over medium-high heat, cook the beef and onion, stirring occasionally, until the beef is browned and crumbly. Drain off excess fat. Turn the beef and onion into a 3½-quart electric slow cooker. Stir in the rice mix (including the dry seasoning packet), water, and 4 tablespoons soy sauce.

2. Cover and cook on the high heat setting 2 hours. Stir the rice mixture. Stir in the chop suey vegetables and mushrooms. Cover and continue cooking on high about ½ hour longer, until the rice is tender and the vegetables are still crisp-tender. Stir in the remaining 1 tablespoon soy sauce and serve at once.

Curried Ground Beef and Rice

Here's your curry and rice all in one. Pass extra chutney and accompany with a cucumber-yogurt salad on a bed of spinach leaves.

MAKES 4 TO 6 SERVINGS

1 pound lean ground beef
1 medium onion, chopped
1 cup converted white rice
1 (28-ounce) can diced peeled
   tomatoes
1½ cups water
2 medium Granny Smith apples, peeled
   and chopped

2 tablespoons Madras curry powder
2 tablespoons raisins
2 tablespoons mango chutney
½ teaspoon garlic powder
½ teaspoon seasoned salt
¼ teaspoon garlic pepper

1. In a large skillet, cook the beef and onion on top of the stove over medium-high heat, stirring occasionally, until the beef is browned and crumbly, 6 to 8 minutes. Drain off any excess fat.

2. Transfer the beef and onion to a 3½-quart electric slow cooker. Add the rice, tomatoes with their liquid, water, apples, curry powder, raisins, chutney, garlic powder, seasoned salt, and garlic pepper. Mix well.

3. Cover and cook on the low heat setting about 3¾ to 4 hours, or until the rice is tender but not mushy. Stir and serve at once.

Easy Meat Sauce

For best-tasting results, brown the ground beef on top of the stove before adding it to the slow cooker. Serve over a pound of spaghetti or your favorite pasta.

MAKES 4 TO 6 SERVINGS

1 pound lean ground beef
1 medium onion, chopped
1 (28-ounce) can diced peeled
  tomatoes
1 (12-ounce) can tomato paste
¾ cup dry red wine
6 carrots, peeled and diced

2 garlic cloves, crushed through a
  press
2 tablespoons dried basil
1 tablespoon Worcestershire sauce
½ teaspoon salt
¼ teaspoon freshly ground pepper

1. In a large skillet on top of the stove, cook the beef and onion over medium-high heat, stirring often, until the beef is browned, 6 to 8 minutes. Drain off excess fat.

2. Transfer the beef and onion to a 3½-quart electric slow cooker. Stir in the tomatoes with their liquid, tomato paste, wine, carrots, garlic, dried basil, Worcestershire sauce, salt, and pepper.

3. Cover and cook on the low heat setting 5 to 6 hours.

Ground Beef and Potato Casserole

This layered casserole is a big hit with teenagers and adults alike. Once the ground beef and onion are browned in a skillet, it's a cinch to assemble the casserole. Consider this easy creation for your next potluck offering.

MAKES 4 TO 5 SERVINGS

1 pound lean ground beef
1 medium onion, chopped
1 (5¼-ounce) package Cheddar and bacon potatoes
1 (15¼-ounce) can whole kernel corn, well drained

1 (10¾-ounce) can condensed cream of potato soup or cream of mushroom soup
1 cup water
3 tablespoons dry sherry
½ cup chopped roasted red peppers
1 (4-ounce) can diced green chiles

1. In a large skillet, cook the beef and onion on top of the stove over medium-high heat, stirring often, until the beef is browned and crumbly, 6 to 8 minutes. Drain off excess fat.

2. Scatter the dried potatoes over the bottom of a 3½-quart electric slow cooker. Sprinkle on the corn. In a medium bowl, whisk together the undiluted soup with the sauce mix packet from the package of potatoes, the water, and sherry until thoroughly blended. Stir in the roasted red peppers and green chiles. Drizzle about a third of this soup mixture over the corn and potatoes (do not mix). Top with the cooked beef and onion. Pour the remaining soup mixture evenly over the top (do not mix).

3. Cover and cook on the low heat setting 4 to 4½ hours, or until the potatoes are tender. Serve at once.

Ground Beef and Sausage with Pasta in Tomato Cream Sauce

This dish has rustic, hearty flavor with both beef and Italian sausage. For a hotter sauce, use more hot Italian sausage than mild. Serve a salad and garlic bread on the side.

MAKES 5 TO 6 SERVINGS

1 pound lean ground beef
¾ pound mild and/or hot Italian sausages, casings removed
2 medium onions, chopped
2 large garlic cloves, minced
1 (26-ounce) jar tomato and basil pasta sauce or spaghetti sauce with mushrooms

1 (14½-ounce) can diced peeled tomatoes
1½ tablespoons dried basil
¼ cup chopped fresh basil
½ cup heavy cream
¾ pound tagliatelle or fettuccine noodles, cooked according to package directions and drained

1. Crumble the beef and sausages into a large heavy skillet on top of the stove. Add the onions and cook over medium-high heat, stirring occasionally, until the meat is well browned, about 8 minutes. Drain off excess fat.
2. Transfer the meat mixture to a 3½-quart electric slow cooker. Stir in the garlic, pasta sauce, tomatoes with their liquid, and dried basil.
3. Cover and cook on the low heat setting 4 to 4½ hours. Stir in the fresh basil and cream. Spoon the sauce over the noodles and toss. Serve at once.

Mexican Beans and Rice with Spicy Meatballs

Here's a one-dish meal that's a surefire hit. Be sure to use extra-lean ground beef in the meatballs so you don't end up with excess fat in this dish. Serve with small bowls of chopped fresh cilantro, sliced scallions, green tomatillo salsa, and sour cream to spoon on top.

MAKES 6 TO 8 SERVINGS

1 pound extra-lean ground beef
2 (1¼-ounce) packages taco seasoning
   mix
½ cup chopped fresh cilantro or
   parsley
½ cup plain bread crumbs
⅓ cup finely chopped carrots
3½ cups water

1 ((2¼-ounce) can sliced ripe olives,
   drained
1 (7-ounce) can diced green chiles
6 garlic cloves, minced
1 red bell pepper, diced
2 cups converted white rice
1 (15-ounce) can kidney beans, rinsed
   and drained

1. To make the meatballs, in a medium bowl, combine the ground beef, ½ package taco seasoning mix, cilantro, bread crumbs, carrots, and ½ cup of the water. Mix to blend well. Roll into 24 balls about 1½ inches in diameter. Set aside.

2. For the beans and rice, in a 4- or 5-quart electric slow cooker, mix together the remaining 3 cups water with the remaining taco seasoning mix, olives, green chiles, garlic, bell pepper, and rice. Gently push the meatballs down into the rice mixture.

3. Cover and cook on the low heat setting 4 hours, or until the rice is just tender and the meatballs are cooked through.

4. Gently stir in the beans. Cover and cook 30 minutes longer.

Picadillo

This Spanish ground meat stew is great party fare. I've substituted dried apricots for the traditional raisins. Double the recipe for a larger group. Use as a filling for tortillas or tacos or serve over steamed rice or orzo. Toasted slivered almonds or pine nuts make an attractive garnish.

MAKES 6 SERVINGS

2 pounds lean ground beef or ground turkey

2 medium onions, chopped

2 garlic cloves, crushed through a press

1 (14½-ounce) can diced peeled tomatoes in puree

1 (8-ounce) can tomato sauce

1 (6-ounce) can tomato paste

½ cup dry sherry

¼ cup balsamic vinegar

⅓ cup chopped dried apricots

½ cup coarsley chopped pimiento-stuffed olives

1½ teaspoons ground cumin

½ teaspoon dried oregano

¼ teaspoon salt

¼ teaspoon freshly ground pepper

1. In a large skillet, cook the beef and onions on top of the stove over medium-high heat, stirring occasionally, until the beef is browned and crumbly, 6 to 8 minutes. Drain off excess fat.

2. Transfer the beef and onions to a 3½-quart electric slow cooker. Add all the remaining ingredients, stirring to blend well.

3. Cover and cook on the low heat setting about 5 to 6 hours. Serve hot.

Slow-Cooker Corned Beef and Cabbage

The slow cooker is the perfect way to go for this traditional dish, since it must bubble away untended for hours in any event. Be sure to serve with crusty bread and pass Dijon mustard and horseradish on the side.

MAKES 6 TO 8 SERVINGS

4 cups hot water
2 tablespoons cider vinegar
2 tablespoons sugar
½ teaspoon freshly ground pepper
1 large or 2 medium onions, cut into wedges
1 (3-pound) corned beef round or brisket packaged with spices

8 small white or yellow potatoes, scrubbed and cut into quarters
1 head of green cabbage (about 1½ pounds), cored and cut into 10 wedges

1. In a 6-quart electric slow cooker, combine the water, vinegar, sugar, pepper, and onions, mixing well. Placed the corned beef in the mixture. Scatter the potatoes over the top and along the sides.

2. Cover and cook on the high heat setting 4 hours. Remove the lid and scatter the cabbage wedges over the top. Cover and continue cooking on high 3 to 4 hours longer, or until the beef is tender. To serve, carve the beef into slices and serve with the cabbage and potatoes, with some of the cooking liquid spooned on top of the beef to keep it moist.

Corned Beef with Dried Fruits and Onions

This aromatic mélange offers a wonderful alternative to traditional corned beef flavors. It can be made a day ahead of time, sliced, and arranged with the fruits, onions, and sauce in a casserole dish. Refrigerate overnight and reheat, covered, in a moderate oven. Serve with coleslaw and crusty rye rolls.

MAKES 6 TO 8 SERVINGS

2 medium onions, thickly sliced

1 (3- to 4-pound) lean corned beef brisket, rinsed several times, patted dry with paper towels, and trimmed of fat

1 cup mixed dried fruits (apples, peaches, prunes, apricots, pears, raisins)

½ cup dried cranberries or cherries

1 (12-ounce) bottle light ale

⅓ cup frozen orange juice concentrate, thawed

½ cup homemade or canned beef broth

¼ cup molasses

Grated zest of 1 large orange

2½ tablespoons cornstarch

3 tablespoons cold water

1. Place half of the onions in a 4- or 5-quart electric slow cooker. Place the corned beef on top, fat side up. Top with the remaining onions. Then sprinkle on the mixed fruits and dried cranberries. Mix together the ale, orange juice concentrate, beef broth, molasses, and orange zest. Carefully pour the liquid over the top of the brisket and down the sides.

2. Cover and cook on the low heat setting 9 to 10 hours, or until the brisket is tender. Remove the corned beef to a carving board. With a slotted spoon, transfer the onions and fruits to a bowl. Strain the juices remaining in the slow cooker into a large glass bowl or a 2-quart glass measure. You should have about 3½ cups (if more, discard). Mix the cornstarch with the cold water until well blended. Stir into the juices. Heat in a microwave oven on high power, 3 to 5 minutes, stopping and stirring a few times, until the sauce boils and is glossy and thickened. (You can also heat the juices in a saucepan on top of the stove over high heat, stirring constantly.)

3. Cut the corned beef into slices across the grain and arrange in a deep platter or casserole dish. Scatter the onions and fruits over the meat and top with some of the sauce. Pass the remaining sauce separately.

Veal Roast with Wild Mushroom Sauce

The earthiness of the mushrooms dominates this elegant creation, which is perfect for a small dinner party. Serve with buttered asparagus and wide egg noodles or wild rice.

MAKES 4 TO 6 SERVINGS

1 ounce dried porcini or imported
    dried mushrooms
½ cup hot water
1 (14½-ounce) can chicken broth
3 tablespoons dry sherry
2 (1½-ounce) packages cream of wild
    mushroom soup mix
½ pound fresh white mushrooms,
    sliced

1 red bell pepper, finely diced
1 small leek (white and tender green),
    rinsed well, trimmed, and thinly
    sliced
2 to 2½ pounds veal shoulder or
    round bone roast (bone in or bone-
    less), trimmed of fat

1. In a small bowl, soak the dried mushrooms in the hot water for almost 20 minutes, until soft. Stir in the chicken broth, sherry, and dry soup mix, mixing well.

2. In a 3½- or 4-quart electric slow cooker, place half each of the sliced mushrooms, bell pepper, and leek. Pour in half of the broth mixture. Place the roast on top and add the remaining sliced mushrooms, bell pepper, and leek. Top with the remaining broth mixture.

3. Cover and cook on the low heat setting 8 to 9 hours, or until the veal is tender.

Curried Lamb with White Beans

Here's a hearty but appealing take on curried lamb. Serve with chutney, peanuts, grated coconut, chopped scallions, and raisins.

MAKES 6 TO 8 SERVINGS

1 (16-ounce) package dried small white beans, rinsed and picked over

2 cups very hot water

1 cup dry white wine

1 red onion, chopped

2 garlic cloves, minced

1 large Granny Smith apple, chopped

½ green bell pepper, chopped

½ red bell pepper, chopped, or ¼ cup chopped roasted red peppers

2 tablespoons plus 1 teaspoon Madras curry powder

1 teaspoon ground cumin

1 teaspoon Beau Monde seasoning

1/4 teaspoon ground turmeric

2 pounds lean boneless lamb stew meat, trimmed of fat and cut into 1½-inch cubes

1. In a 4-quart electric slow cooker, combine the beans, hot water, wine, red onion, garlic, apple, green and red bell peppers, 2 tablespoons of the curry powder, the cumin, Beau Monde seasoning, and turmeric. Add the lamb and mix well.

2. Cover and cook on the high heat setting 1 hour. Reduce the heat setting to low. Cook, covered, on low 5½ to 6½ hours longer, or until the beans are tender but not mushy. Stir in the remaining 1 teaspoon curry powder.

Chili Verde

Although black beans are not traditional in chili verde, they make the dish a little more substantial and add texture. Garnish with fresh cilantro and lime wedges and serve with warm tortillas. Also, try the mixture as a burrito filling.

MAKES 6 TO 8 SERVINGS

2 pounds lean boneless pork, cut into
    thin strips or ¾-inch cubes
3 tablespoons all-purpose flour
1 cup water
2 tablespoons ground cumin
¾ teaspoon chili powder
½ teaspoon dried oregano
½ teaspoon garlic pepper

½ teaspoon seasoned salt
3 medium onions, thinly sliced
2 (7-ounce) cans whole green chiles,
    rinsed, drained, and cut into strips
¾ cup roasted red pepper strips
1 (15-ounce) can black beans, rinsed
    and drained (optional)

1. In a 3½-quart electric slow cooker, toss the pork with the flour until evenly coated. Stir in the water, cumin, chili powder, oregano, garlic pepper, seasoned salt, onions, and half of the chile strips. Mix well.

2. Cover and cook on the low heat setting about 6 hours, stirring twice, if possible, or until the pork is very tender. Increase the heat setting to high.

3. Stir in the remaining chile strips, the red pepper strips, and the black beans. Cover and cook on high 20 to 30 minutes longer, until heated through.

Barbecued Pork and Potatoes

This is a breeze to prepare and the end results are delicious. Serve with coleslaw.

MAKES 5 TO 6 SERVINGS

6 medium russet potatoes, peeled and
    cut into 1½-inch cubes (about 1¾
    pounds)
2 pounds boneless pork loin, trimmed
    of fat and cut into 1-inch cubes

1 teaspoon dry mustard
2 cups prepared hickory-flavored
    barbecue sauce
Salt and freshly ground pepper

1. Place the potatoes in a 4-quart electric slow cooker. Top with the pork cubes. Mix the mustard into 1 cup of the barbecue sauce. Spoon evenly over the pork and potatoes.

2. Cover and cook on the low heat setting 8 to 9 hours, or until the potatoes and pork are tender. Stir in the remaining 1 cup barbecue sauce. Season with salt and pepper to taste.

Barbecued Country Ribs

Simmer meaty country-style pork ribs in a tasty sauce made quickly with prepared barbecue sauce, apricot-pineapple jam, and a little soy sauce. Be sure to trim the ribs of as much fat as possible before adding them to the slow cooker. For added color, you can bake the ribs in a single layer in a shallow pan in a 450 degree F oven for about ½ hour, until well browned, before adding them to the slow cooker; if you do this, decrease the cooking time by about 1 hour.

MAKES 6 SERVINGS

1½ cups prepared hickory-flavored
   barbecue sauce
½ cup apricot-pineapple jam

1 tablespoon soy sauce
3¾ to 4 pounds boneless country-style
   pork spareribs, trimmed of fat

1. In a medium bowl, mix together ¾ cup barbecue sauce, the jam, and soy sauce until well blended. Place a layer of the ribs in a 4-quart electric slow cooker. Pour on ⅓ of the sauce mixture. Top with another layer of ribs and half of the remaining sauce. Top with the remaining ribs and pour on the remaining sauce.
2. Cover and cook on the low heat setting 8½ to 9 hours, or until the ribs are tender but not completely falling apart.
3. Remove the ribs to a serving dish. Skim off and discard any fat from the sauce in the slow cooker. Stir in the remaining ¾ cup barbecue sauce. Pass the sauce to spoon over the ribs.

NOTE: For a thicker sauce to serve with the ribs, discard half of the sauce remaining in the slow cooker before adding the remaining ¾ cup barbecue sauce.

Red-Cooked Ribs

In Chinese cooking, red cooking refers to the method of braising foods in soy sauce and other dark-colored ingredients, which often turns the foods a reddish brown. These saucy ribs are succulent and tasty. Serve with steamed rice and broccoli.

MAKES 6 SERVINGS

¾ cup hoisin sauce

3 tablespoons dark soy sauce

2 tablespoons dry sherry

1 tablespoon minced fresh ginger

1 tablespoon honey

5 garlic cloves, minced

1 teaspoon ground allspice

1 tablespoon grated orange zest

½ to 1 teaspoon crushed hot red pepper

6 scallions, cut diagonally into 1-inch pieces

1 (8-ounce) can sliced water chestnuts, drained

3 pounds country-style pork ribs, trimmed of fat

1. In a small bowl, mix together the hoisin sauce, soy sauce, sherry, ginger, honey, garlic, allspice, orange zest, and hot pepper.

2. Place ⅓ of the scallions and water chestnut slices in a 3½-quart electric slow cooker. Top with some of the ribs and spoon some of the sauce on the meat. Repeat these layers 2 more times, ending with the remaining sauce.

3. Cover and cook on the low heat setting 9 to 10 hours, or until the ribs are tender.

Ham and Pineapple Bean Pot

When you want an easy potluck offering, throw these ingredients into your slow cooker. It's a good way to use up leftover ham.

MAKES 4 TO 5 SERVINGS

2 (15-ounce) cans pinto beans, rinsed and drained

1 (15-ounce) can black beans, rinsed and drained

1 (15½-ounce) can Texas-style barbecue beans with their liquid

1 (20-ounce) can unsweetened pineapple chunks

⅓ cup prepared hickory-flavored barbecue sauce

2 tablespoons prepared yellow mustard

1 medium onion, chopped

1 medium green pepper, chopped

1 pound cooked smoked ham, cut into ¾-inch cubes

2 tablespoons red wine vinegar

Freshly ground pepper

1. In a 3½- or 4-quart electric slow cooker, combine the beans, drained pineapple chunks, barbecue sauce, mustard, onion, green pepper, and ham. Mix gently.

2. Cover and cook on the low heat setting 5½ to 6 hours (the onion and green pepper will still be crunchy). Stir in the vinegar and season with pepper to taste.

Easy Ham and Potato Hash

Whether you serve it with scrambled eggs and English muffins for brunch or with whole-grain bread and a tossed salad for supper, this is a delicious, no-fuss way to use leftover ham. Note: If you forget to take the potatoes out of the freezer, microwave them on high power for 4 minutes, until barely thawed.

MAKES 6 SERVINGS

1 (32-ounce) package frozen hash brown potatoes, partially thawed
¾ cup chopped green bell pepper
¾ cup chopped red bell pepper
3 cups chopped cooked ham
1 (8-ounce) package cream cheese, softened

1½ cups milk
2½ tablespoons Dijon mustard
1½ cups chopped scallions
½ teaspoon garlic powder
½ teaspoon garlic pepper

1. In a 4-quart electric slow cooker, combine the hash brown potatoes with the red and green bell peppers and ham. Stir to mix well. In a 1-quart glass measure, blend the cream cheese and milk. Heat in a microwave oven on high power 1 to 1½ minutes, or until smooth when whisked together. Stir in the mustard, 1 cup of the scallions, the garlic powder, and pepper until blended. Pour this cream cheese mixture evenly over the potatoes and ham; do not mix.

2. Cover and cook on the low heat setting 5 to 6 hours, or until the potatoes are tender. Stir gently. Sprinkle the remaining ½ cup scallions over the top and serve.

Sweet-and-Sour Cabbage Rolls

These are delicious and might remind you of your grandmother's cooking. Substitute cooked ground beef for the ham, if you prefer.

MAKES 4 TO 6 SERVINGS

1 large head of green cabbage (about 2 pounds)

3 cups ground cooked ham (see Note)

4 scallions, finely chopped

3 tablespoons converted white rice

½ teaspoon freshly ground pepper

1 (28-ounce) can diced peeled tomatoes

1 (6-ounce) can tomato paste

⅓ cup fresh lemon juice

⅓ cup packed brown sugar

⅓ cup golden or dark raisins

1. Rinse and core the cabbage. Carefully remove 8 large outer leaves from the cabbage. In a large pot of boiling water, boil these cabbage leaves about 5 to 7 minutes, or just until limp. Remove and drain well on paper towels.

2. Meanwhile, shred or chop the remaining cabbage and place in the bottom of a 5-quart electric slow cooker. In a medium bowl, combine the ground ham, scallions, rice, and pepper. In a separate bowl, mix together the tomatoes with their liquid and the tomato paste until thoroughly blended. Stir ½ cup of the tomato mixture into the ham and rice.

3. Arrange the cabbage leaves on a flat surface with the stem toward you. Divide the ham mixture evenly among the 8 leaves, placing it near the stem end. Fold in the sides of the cabbage leaves over the meat and carefully roll up.

4. Place the filled cabbage rolls on top of the shredded cabbage in the slow cooker. Stir the lemon juice, brown sugar, and raisins into the remaining tomato mixture and spoon over the top of the rolls and alongside so it seeps into the bottom of the cooker.

5. Cover and cook on the low heat setting 6 to 7 hours, or until the rice in the rolls is tender (the rolls should still be intact and not falling apart). Carefully remove the cooked rolls and serve with the shredded cabbage and sauce.

NOTE: To grind the ham easily, cut it into 1-inch chunks and place in a food processor. Process in pulses just until ground; do not puree to a paste.

Shrimp Jambalaya

Shrimp, ham, and artichokes make this Louisiana Creole classic exceptionally appealing.

1½ cups converted white rice
1 (28-ounce) can diced peeled
  tomatoes
¾ cup dry white wine
3 celery ribs, chopped
2 medium onions, chopped
1 green or yellow bell pepper, chopped
1 (13¾-ounce) can quartered artichoke
  hearts, rinsed and well drained
3 tablespoons chopped fresh parsley

½ teaspoon garlic powder
⅛ to ¼ teaspoon cayenne
¼ teaspoon seasoned salt
½ teaspoon freshly ground black
  pepper
¼ cup chopped fresh basil or 1
  teaspoon dried
1 cup chopped cooked ham
¾ to 1 pound peeled and deveined
  cooked shrimp

1. In a 3½- or 4-quart electric slow cooker, mix together the rice, tomatoes with their liquid, wine, celery, onions, bell pepper, artichokes, parsley, garlic powder, cayenne, seasoned salt, and black pepper.

2. Cover and cook on the low heat setting 3½ to 4 hours, or until the rice is tender but not sticky and mushy. Stir in the basil, ham, and shrimp. Cook, covered, 10 to 15 minutes longer, or until the ham and shrimp are hot.

Coconut Thai Shrimp and Rice

This slightly spicy, slightly sweet complex combination of Asian flavors will please the pickiest eaters. Adjust the heat by adding more or less cayenne, depending on your own taste.

2 (14½-ounce) cans chicken broth
1 cup water
1 teaspoon ground coriander
1 teaspoon ground cumin
1 teaspoon salt
½ to ¾ teaspoon cayenne
Grated zest and juice of 2 limes
    (⅓ cup lime juice)
7 garlic cloves, minced
1 tablespoon minced fresh ginger
1 medium onion, chopped

1 red bell pepper, diced
1 carrot, peeled and shredded
¼ cup flaked coconut
½ cup golden raisins
2 cups converted white rice
1 pound peeled and deveined cooked
    jumbo shrimp, thawed if frozen
2 ounces fresh snow peas, cut into
    thin strips
Toasted coconut, for garnish

1. In a 4- or 5-quart electric slow cooker, mix the chicken broth, water, coriander, cumin, salt, cayenne, lime zest, lime juice, garlic, and ginger. Stir in the onion, bell pepper, carrot, coconut, raisins, and rice.
2. Cover and cook on the low heat setting 3½ hours, or until the rice is just tender.
3. Stir in the shrimp and snow peas. Cover and cook 30 minutes longer. Serve garnished with toasted coconut.

Chapter Six
Meatless Main Courses

In the interest of health, more and more Americans now favor including meatless meals in their menus once, twice, or even several times a week. That means relying more on legumes, vegetables, fruits, grains, and in some instances, dairy products. For those desiring meals without meat, there are plenty of delicious and appealing slow-cooker options: vegetable curries, vegetable or bean chilis, bean salads, and garden-style tomato sauces to serve over pasta or polenta, to name just a few.

Beans are inexpensive and a nutritional bargain, low in fat, rich in protein and fiber, and cholesterol free. Several standard varieties—black, white, lima, garbanzo, pinto, small red, kidney, and Great Northern—are readily available in supermarkets, along with some of the newer specialty varieties such as Anasazi, cranberry, and scarlet runners.

I'm convinced that the slow cooker is one of, if not *the*, best ways to cook dried beans. Regardless of what the package says, no presoaking or precooking of the beans is required. That means you don't have to plan ahead. Simply rinse, drain, and pick over a pound of dried beans, discarding any debris or foreign particles and place in a 3½-quart slow cooker. Cover with 5 cups of very hot water (from the tap is fine), cover the pot, and turn the heat setting to low. In 5 to 7 hours (depending on the type and age of the beans), they should be tender but still hold their shape. If you're planning to mash or puree the beans, cook them until they are a little softer. If you're in a hurry, the beans can also be cooked on the high heat setting for about 3 to 4 hours.

The range in cooking times depends on the age of the beans, their water content, where they were grown, and the season in which they were harvested. Generally, the older the bean, the longer the required cooking time. Bean packages often include use by date information which is helpful, so check packages prior to purchasing.

Figure that a pound (about 2 cups) of dried beans will yield anywhere from 5½ to 7½ cups of cooked beans. Cooked beans can be refrigerated for 2 to 3 days or frozen for up to 2 months for use in soups, chilis, and salads.

Uncooked dried beans can also be cooked simultaneously with other ingredients in the slow cooker to make hearty one-dish meals. Contrary to popular belief, I found you can add salt and acidic ingredients like tomatoes at the beginning of the cooking time and still end up with tender, digestible beans.

Of the many appealing vegetable main dishes in this chapter, some, such as Ratatouille and Vegetable Chili, can be eaten on their own, topped with cheese if you like, or used as a base for salads when you want a lighter meal. You can also, effortlessly, without tending, whip up sauces to serve over hot cooked pastas. Once again, the slow cooker shows off its versatility as it lends itself to a variety of eating styles.

Black Bean Chili

The cooking time of black beans can vary a great deal depending on how long they were stored and where they were grown. With the same slow-cooker technique, black beans have at different times taken as little as 5½ or 6 hours on low or as long as 9 hours on the same heat setting; so start checking after 5 or 6 hours, but leave yourself some extra time, just in case. I like to top this meatless chili with shredded lettuce and carrots, chopped tomatoes, scallions, and avocado, and a dollop of sour cream or yogurt.

MAKES 5 TO 6 SERVINGS

1 (16-ounce) package dried black beans, rinsed and picked over
4 cups boiling water
1 large onion, chopped
1 green bell pepper, cut into 1-inch squares
1 red bell pepper, cut into 1-inch squares
1½ tablespoons chili powder
1½ tablespoons ground cumin
¼ teaspoon seasoned salt
3 garlic cloves, minced
½ teaspoon liquid smoke hickory seasoning
1 (6-ounce) can tomato paste
6 large plum tomatoes, chopped, or 1 (28-ounce) can Italian peeled tomatoes, drained and chopped

1. In a 3½-quart electric slow cooker, mix together the beans, water, onion, green and red bell peppers, chili powder, cumin, seasoned salt, garlic, and liquid smoke.
2. Cover and cook on the low heat setting 6 to 9 hours, or until the beans are tender. Stir in the tomato paste and tomatoes.

Vegetarian Enchilada Casserole

Stick to corn tortillas here as they yield a more desirable result than the flour variety, which falls apart in the slow cooker. For best results, don't cook beyond the time recommended in the recipe. Sprinkle shredded Cheddar or Monterey Jack cheese over the top, if you like, just before serving.

MAKES 5 TO 6 SERVINGS

1 (28-ounce) can crushed tomatoes in tomato puree
1 (14½-ounce) can chunky salsa
1 (6-ounce) can tomato paste
2 (15-ounce) cans black beans, rinsed and drained
1 (15¼-ounce) can whole kernel corn, drained

1 (4-ounce) can diced green chiles
1½ tablespoons ground cumin
½ teaspoon garlic powder
5 corn tortillas
1 (2¼-ounce) can sliced ripe olives, drained

1. In a large bowl, combine the tomatoes, salsa, tomato paste, beans, corn, green chiles, cumin, and garlic powder. Mix well. Ladle about 1 cup of this mixture in to the bottom of a 4-quart electric slow cooker; spread evenly. Top with 1½ tortillas, cutting to fit as necessary. Spread on ⅓ of the remaining tomato mixture. Repeat these layers 2 more times, ending with the rest of the tomato mixture; spread evenly over the top. Sprinkle the sliced olives over all.

2. Cover and cook on the low heat setting about 5 hours. Serve hot.

Stuffed Peppers

These rice and vegetable stuffed peppers are versatile: whole peppers can be presented as a colorful main dish, halves as a vegetable accompaniment to grilled meats or fish.

MAKES 4 MAIN-COURSE OR 8 SIDE-DISH SERVINGS

2 large green bell peppers
2 large red bell peppers
½ cup converted white rice
1 (15¼-ounce) can whole kernel corn, drained
1 (2¼-ounce) can sliced ripe olives, drained

3 scallions, chopped
¼ teaspoon seasoned salt
¼ teaspoon garlic pepper
1 (14½-ounce) can cut-up peeled tomatoes
⅓ cup dry red wine
1 (6-ounce) can tomato paste

1. Slice the tops off the green and red bell peppers and carefully remove the seeds and inner ribs. Remove the stems from the tops and chop the remaining pepper pieces. Stand the peppers upright in a 5-quart electric slow cooker.

2. In a medium bowl, combine the chopped pepper tops, rice, corn, olives, scallions, seasoned salt, garlic pepper, and ½ cup of the tomatoes with their liquid. Mix well. Stuff the peppers with the corn mixture, dividing evenly and packing lightly. Mix the remaining tomatoes and their liquid with the wine and tomato paste until well blended. Pour over and around the peppers in the slow cooker.

3. Cover and cook on the low heat setting 6½ to 7 hours, or until the rice is cooked and the peppers are tender but still hold their shape.

Ratatouille

Make a whole meal of this French vegetarian classic while it's warm or offer it chilled as a salad course. Serve with crusty bread and top with crumbled feta cheese, if you like.

MAKES 6 TO 8 SERVINGS

1 large eggplant, peeled and cut into 1-inch chunks

Salt

2 medium onions, chopped

2 cups chopped fresh tomatoes (about 3 medium)

1 large green bell pepper, cut into ½-inch squares

1 large red or yellow bell pepper, cut into ½-inch squares

3 medium zucchini, sliced

3 tablespoons olive oil

3 tablespoons dried basil

2 garlic cloves, crushed through a press

½ teaspoon freshly ground pepper

1 (6-ounce) can tomato paste

1 (5¾-ounce) can pitted ripe olives, drained and coarsely chopped

3 tablespoons chopped fresh basil

1. Sprinkle the eggplant with salt; let stand in a colander ½ to 1 hour to drain. Press out excess moisture. Rinse the eggplant with water and pat dry with paper towels.

2. Place the eggplant in a 5- or 6-quart electric slow cooker. Add the onions, tomatoes, bell peppers, zucchini, olive oil, basil, garlic, pepper, and ½ teaspoon salt. Mix well.

3. Cover and cook on the high heat setting about 3 hours, until the vegetables are tender but still hold their shape. Stir in the tomato paste, olives, and fresh basil. Serve hot, at room temperature, or chilled.

Rice, Corn, and Spinach Casserole

This savory dish doubles as a vegetarian main course or a side dish to serve with grilled meats or chicken.

MAKES 6 TO 8 SERVINGS

1 (10-ounce) package frozen chopped spinach, partially thawed but not drained

1½ cups converted white rice

1 (10¾-ounce) can cream of mushroom soup

2 cups water

1 (4-ounce) can diced green chiles

1 (15¼-ounce) can whole kernel corn, drained

½ teaspoon garlic powder

1 cup shredded sharp Cheddar cheese

1. In a 3½- or 4-quart electric slow cooker, combine the undrained spinach, rice, undiluted soup, water, chiles, corn, and garlic powder. Mix well.

2. Cover and cook on the high heat setting 2 to 2¼ hours, or just until the rice is tender but not mushy.

3. Sprinkle the cheese on top, cover, and cook 5 minutes longer, or until the cheese is melted. Serve immediately.

Tortellini with Broccoli

This is one recipe that you don't want to overcook, or you'll end up with mush. Serve a salad and Italian bread on the side.

MAKES 4 SERVINGS

1 (26-ounce) jar tomato and basil pasta sauce
1 (9-ounce) package fresh spinach and three-cheese tortellini (available in the refrigerator section of supermarkets)

1 tablespoon dried basil
1 (16-ounce) package frozen cut broccoli spears

1. In a 3½- or 4-quart electric slow cooker, place about ½ cup of the pasta sauce. Top evenly with all the tortellini. Add half of the remaining sauce, sprinkle on the basil and then all of the frozen broccoli. Top with the remaining sauce.
2. Cover and cook on the high heat setting 2¾ to 3 hours. Do not overcook, or the pasta will lose its shape and become mushy. Serve immediately.

Garden Fresh Tomato Sauce

When your summer garden is overflowing with fresh-from-the-vine tomatoes, use the slow cooker to whip up several batches of this sauce to stash in the freezer. If you don't grow your own, try Roma tomatoes from the market. Serve over your favorite pasta, grilled vegetables, chicken, or fish.

MAKES ABOUT 7 CUPS

3½ to 4 pounds ripe tomatoes, peeled and chopped
1 (6-ounce) can tomato paste
½ cup dry white wine
1 large red onion, chopped
1 tablespoon extra-virgin olive oil
4 large garlic cloves, minced

2 teaspoons dried basil
¼ teaspoon dried oregano
½ teaspoon salt
¼ teaspoon freshly ground pepper
½ teaspoon sugar, or to taste
1 tablespoon balsamic vinegar
¼ cup chopped fresh basil

1. In a 3½- or 4-quart electric slow cooker, mix together the tomatoes, tomato paste, wine, red onion, olive oil, garlic, dried basil, oregano, salt, and pepper.
2. Cover and cook on the low heat setting 4 to 4½ hours.
3. Stir in the sugar, vinegar, and fresh basil. Increase the heat setting to high and cook, uncovered, ½ hour longer to thicken the sauce slightly.

MUSHROOM SAUCE: Along with the sugar, vinegar, and fresh basil, stir in 1 ounce dried porcini mushrooms that have been rinsed quickly under running tap water and coarsely chopped. Cover and cook on the high heat setting 30 to 40 minutes longer, or until the mushrooms are soft.

PUTTANESCA SAUCE: Along with the sugar, vinegar, and fresh basil, stir in ¼ cup drained capers and ¾ cup coarsely chopped pitted kalamata olives.

Tomato Mushroom Sauce

Try this sauce over steamed zucchini or spaghetti squash as well as on your favorite pasta.

MAKES ABOUT 9 CUPS

1 (28-ounce) can crushed tomatoes with puree
1 (28-ounce) can diced peeled tomatoes
1 (6-ounce) can tomato paste
1 medium onion, chopped
2 garlic cloves, crushed through a press

1 tablespoon dried basil
½ teaspoon dried oregano
¼ teaspoon freshly ground pepper
½ pound fresh white mushrooms, sliced
½ teaspoon sugar
Salt

1. In a 3½-quart electric slow cooker, mix together the crushed tomatoes, diced tomatoes with their liquid, tomato paste, onion, garlic, basil, oregano, pepper, and mushrooms.

2. Cover and cook on the low heat setting 6½ to 7 hours. Mix in the sugar and season with salt to taste.

Vegetable Chili

When you want a lighter version of chili, try this variation. Chopping the vegetables takes a little time, but after turning everything into the slow cooker, the machine does all the work. Serve over brown rice and top with a little shredded cheese and plain nonfat yogurt.

MAKES 4 TO 5 SERVINGS

2 medium zucchini, chopped
1 medium red bell pepper, chopped
1 medium green bell pepper, chopped
3 carrots, peeled and chopped
3 celery ribs, chopped
2 medium onions, chopped
2 large tomatoes, chopped, or 1 (14½-ounce) can Italian peeled tomatoes, drained and chopped
1 (15¼-ounce) can whole kernel corn, well drained

1 (15¼-ounce) can garbanzo beans (chick-peas), rinsed and well drained
2 teaspoons chili powder
2 teaspoons ground cumin
1 (15-ounce) can mild salsa
⅓ cup tomato paste
Salt and pepper

1. In a 4-quart electric slow cooker, mix together the zucchini, bell peppers, carrots, celery, onions, tomatoes, corn, garbanzo beans, chili powder, cumin, and salsa.
2. Cover and cook on the low heat setting about 8 hours, or until the vegetables are almost tender.
3. Stir in the tomato paste. Season with salt and pepper to taste.

Vegetable Curry

Served over rice, this fragrant, spicy stew provides an excellent vegetarian meal. Pass chutney, whole wheat pita bread, and shredded cucumber mixed with plain yogurt on the side.

MAKES 4 TO 6 SERVINGS

4 medium russet potatoes (about 1¾ pounds), peeled and cut into ½-inch dice

1 large onion, chopped

1 red bell pepper, chopped

2 carrots, peeled and cut into ½-inch dice

2 large plum tomatoes, chopped

1 (6-ounce) can tomato paste

¾ cup water

2 tablespoons curry powder

2 teaspoons cumin seeds

½ teaspoon garlic powder

½ teaspoon salt

1 medium head of cauliflower, cut into 1-inch florets

1 (10-ounce) package frozen peas or cut green beans, thawed

1. In a 4- or 5-quart electric slow cooker, toss together the potatoes, onion, bell pepper, carrots, and tomatoes. Stir in the tomato paste, water, curry powder, cumin seeds, garlic powder, and salt. Mix well. Place the cauliflower florets on top.

2. Cover and cook on the low heat setting 8 to 9 hours, or until the potatoes are tender but still hold their shape. Gently stir in the peas. Increase the heat to the high setting and cook 15 minutes longer.

Vegetable Paella

This is one slow-cooker dish you have to pay attention to near the end, because overcooking will turn the rice into mush. Serve as a vegetarian main course or as a side dish with chicken, sausage, or shrimp.

MAKES 6 TO 8 SERVINGS

1 (10-ounce) package frozen chopped spinach, thawed but not drained

2 cups converted white rice

4 cups homemade vegetable stock or 2 (14½-ounce) cans vegetable broth

1 green bell pepper, chopped

¾ cup chopped roasted red peppers

1 large onion, chopped

2 garlic cloves, minced

½ teaspoon saffron threads

½ teaspoon salt

¼ teaspoon freshly ground pepper

1 (13¾-ounce) can quartered artichoke hearts, rinsed and well drained

1 (16-ounce) package frozen mixed vegetables, thawed

1. In a 3½- or 4-quart electric slow cooker, combine the undrained spinach, rice, stock, bell pepper, roasted peppers, onion, garlic, saffron, salt, and pepper.

2. Cover and cook on the low heat setting about 4 hours, or until the rice is just tender but the grains are still separate and not mushy; watch closely near the end of the cooking time.

3. Stir in the artichokes and thawed vegetables. Increase the heat to the high setting and cook, uncovered, 10 minutes longer. Serve immediately.

Vegetable-Tomato Sauce

When your garden or farmer's market is overloaded with zucchini and red ripe tomatoes is the time to make this easy sauce. Make several batches, if you like, and freeze for another time. Serve over your favorite pasta, with grated Parmesan or Romano cheese on the side.

MAKES ABOUT 5 CUPS

3 cups packed shredded zucchini
1 pound plum tomatoes, chopped
1 medium onion, chopped
1 red or green bell pepper, chopped
¼ cup dry red wine

2 garlic cloves, minced
1 (6-ounce) can tomato paste
¼ cup chopped fresh basil
Salt and freshly ground pepper

1. In a 3½- or 4-quart electric slow cooker, mix together the zucchini, tomatoes, onion, bell pepper, wine, garlic, and tomato paste.
2. Cover and cook on the low heat setting about 7 hours.
3. Stir in the fresh basil. Season with salt and pepper to taste.

Chapter Seven

Side Dishes and Condiments

The slow cooker lends itself to the preparation of a wealth of interesting side dishes—vegetables, beans, rice dishes, and relishes. Until I began developing recipes for this volume, I had no idea what a tasty challenge it was.

What's particularly nice is that you can walk away from the kitchen, letting the dishes simmer away lazily while you concentrate on other tasks, and then return several hours later to a wonderful finished dish. In most cases, no stirring or watching is required. Even relishes, chutneys, and vegetables, which can scorch, splatter, boil over, or even boil away on top of the stove, are carefree in the slow cooker.

What a pleasure to make Lazy Apricot Preserves, Dried Fruit Chutney, and Pineapple Mango Chutney in a slow cooker. There's no muss and no fuss; it's one-pot cooking at its best. Any one or all three would make great holiday gifts, and they're easy because all use ingredients readily available in the markets all year round. Come holiday time whip up a batch of Cranberry Orange Relish to serve on Thanksgiving. Make it up a week in advance and refrigerate.

The essence of simplicity but great taste can be found in Potatoes with Fresh Fennel, which requires five or six hours of cooking time in a slow cooker. Try it hot as a vegetable or cold as a salad course, drizzled with a little olive oil. Vegetables Agro Dolce is an appetizer offering that is good warm or cold, as is Potatoes, Peppers, and Tomatoes, which can double as a vegetarian main dish when topped with crumbled feta cheese.

Other side dishes, such as Red Cabbage and Apples, Baked Beans, BBQ Cowboy Pinto Beans, and Creamed Corn, are downright old-fashioned comfort fare. Many of these selections would make good contributions to potluck gatherings. And if it's more upscale fare you're seeking, try Rice with Porcini Mushrooms, Asparagus Vegetable Medley, and Green Beans, Peppers, and Tomatoes with Balsamic Vinegar and Sun-Dried Tomatoes.

When cooking a combination of vegetables in a slow cooker, keep in mind that as on top of the stove, the firmer ones will take longer to cook than the softer ones. To even out the cooking time, cut the firmer ones into smaller pieces. And because moisture will build up in the pot, remember that only a small amount of liquid is added.

Asparagus Vegetable Medley

This makes a terrific warm vegetable or chilled salad. It's a great way to use asparagus in season, when it is plentiful and a good buy. For an extra fillip, top with shavings of imported Parmesan cheese.

2 pounds asparagus, cut crosswise on the diagonal into 1-inch pieces

2 large leeks (white part only), rinsed well, halved lengthwise, and sliced

1 green bell pepper, cut into thin strips

1 red bell pepper, cut into thin strips

⅓ cup homemade or canned chicken or vegetable broth

¼ cup red or white wine vinegar

2½ teaspoons dried dill weed

1½ teaspoons dried tarragon, crushed

1 to 2 tablespoons extra-virgin olive oil

1. In a 3½-quart electric slow cooker, mix together the asparagus, leeks, green and red bell peppers, broth, 3 tablespoons of the vinegar, 2 teaspoons of the dill weed, and 1 teaspoon of the tarragon.

2. Cover and cook on the low heat setting 5 to 5½ hours, or until the asparagus is tender but still slightly crisp.

3. Drain off and discard the cooking liquid. Mix in the remaining 1 tablespoon vinegar, ½ teaspoon dill weed, and ½ teaspoon tarragon. Add olive oil to taste. Serve immediately or refrigerate and serve chilled.

Beans Slow Cooker Style

Whether your dried beans are white, black, red, or spotted, the slow cooker is the way to cook them effortlessly. Best of all, no presoaking is required. Cooking time will vary depending upon the size of the bean, how long it's been stored, and even where the bean was originally grown; so it's a good idea to begin checking after 3 hours on high or 5 hours on low. Store the cooked beans in the refrigerator for 2 or 3 days. You can throw the beans into soups or stews, refry them, toss them with pasta, or try one of my salads, which follow.

MAKES 6 TO 8 SERVINGS (6 TO 7 CUPS)

1 (16-ounce) package dried beans, rinsed and picked over

5 cups very hot tap water

1. In a 3½-quart electric slow cooker, combine the beans and hot water.
2. Cover and cook on the high heat setting 3 to 4 hours (or on the low heat setting 5 to 7 hours), until the beans are tender but not falling apart.
3. Drain the beans into a colander and rinse with cold water. Drain well before using.

MEDITERRANEAN WHITE BEAN SALAD: In a medium bowl, combine 3½ cups cooked small white beans with ¼ cup red wine vinegar. Stir in 3 tablespoons chopped roasted red peppers, 2 tablespoons drained capers, 1 garlic clove, crushed through a press, and ¼ teaspoon each salt and freshly ground pepper. In a mini food processor, combine ½ cup well-drained pimiento-stuffed olives, 2 tablespoons extra-virgin olive oil, and 3 tablespoons packed fresh basil. Process until the basil is finely chopped. Pour over the bean salad and toss gently to coat. Serve at room temperature or slightly chilled. Makes 6 to 8 appetizer or 4 salad servings.

TUSCAN TUNA AND BEAN SALAD: In a medium bowl, combine 3½ cups cooked small white beans, 2 chopped tomatoes, 1 (6⅛-ounce) can well-drained solid white tuna, 3 tablespoons each fresh lemon juice and wine vinegar, 2 tablespoons olive oil, 3 tablespoons chopped fresh basil or parsley, 1 garlic clove, crushed through a press, 2 chopped scallions, and ¼ teaspoon each salt and freshly ground pepper. Toss gently to mix. Serve at room temperature or slightly chilled. Makes 4 servings.

BLACK BEAN, CORN, AND TOMATO SALAD: In a large bowl, combine 1 pound black beans, cooked (about 6 cups), 3 chopped large tomatoes, 2 chopped large bell peppers (preferably 1 red, 1 green), 4 chopped scallions, 2 cups corn kernels, ⅓ cup red wine vinegar, ⅓ cup olive oil, and 1½ teaspoons ground cumin. Season with salt and freshly ground pepper to taste. Stir in ¼ cup chopped cilantro, if you have it. Serve at room temperature or slightly chilled. Makes 12 servings.

Baked Beans

Making a pot full of beans in a slow cooker can't get much easier. Serve these at your next casual party, indoors or out.

MAKES 8 TO 10 SERVINGS

2 (15-ounce) cans pinto beans, rinsed and well drained

2 (15-ounce) cans dark red kidney beans, rinsed and well drained

1 (30-ounce) can chili beans, drained (no need to rinse)

1 large onion, chopped

1 medium green bell pepper, coarsely chopped

¾ cup ketchup

1 tablespoon prepared yellow mustard

1 teaspoon liquid smoke hickory seasoning

½ cup packed light brown sugar

2 heaping teaspoons instant coffee powder dissolved in 2 tablespoons boiling water

1. In a 4-quart electric slow cooker, combine the pinto beans, kidney beans, chili beans, onion, and bell pepper. Mix together the ketchup, mustard, liquid smoke, brown sugar, and coffee. Pour over the beans and mix together gently to avoid crushing the beans.

2. Cover and cook on the low heat setting 4 to 5 hours. Mix well. Serve hot.

Boston Baked Bean Pot

For best results and to speed the slow cooker cooking time, here I cook the beans on top of the stove first for a short time before adding to the slow cooker.

MAKES 8 TO 10 SERVINGS

1 (16-ounce) package dried Great Northern or small white beans, rinsed and picked over
8 cups very hot water
⅓ cup dark rum
½ cup molasses
⅓ cup packed brown sugar

2 teaspoons dry mustard
1 medium onion, chopped
¼ teaspoon freshly ground pepper
¼ pound salt pork, rind removed, pork chopped
Salt

1. In a large pot or saucepan, combine the beans and 6 cups of the hot water. Heat to boiling on top of the stove over high heat. Reduce the heat to medium and cook 10 minutes; drain.

2. Add the beans to a 3½-quart electric slow cooker. Add the remaining 2 cups hot water, the rum, molasses, brown sugar, mustard, onion, pepper, and salt pork. Mix well.

3. Cover and cook on the high heat setting 5 to 6 hours, or until the beans are tender. Season with salt to taste and serve.

BBQ Cowboy Pinto Beans

These delicious beans appeal to diners of all ages. Serve with grilled sausages, steaks, or poultry.

MAKES 6 TO 8 SERVINGS

1 (16-ounce) package dried pinto
  beans, rinsed and picked over
4 cups hot water
2 medium onions, chopped
1 tablespoon chili powder
¾ cup hickory-flavored barbecue sauce

½ cup ketchup
1½ tablespoons prepared yellow
  mustard
Dash of Tabasco sauce, or more to
  taste

1. In a 3½-quart electric slow cooker, mix together the beans, hot water, onions, and chili powder.

2. Cover and cook on the low heat setting about 7 hours, or until the beans are tender but not falling apart.

3. Drain off all the cooking liquid. Stir in the barbecue sauce, ketchup, mustard, and Tabasco sauce. Cook, uncovered, 10 to 15 minutes longer, until heated through.

Orange-Glazed Carrots

For convenience and to speed preparation time, purchase peeled baby carrots in plastic bags, which are often sold in supermarket produce departments.

MAKES 8 SERVINGS

1 (32-ounce) package peeled baby carrots
⅓ cup thawed frozen orange juice concentrate
3 tablespoons brown sugar
½ teaspoon ground cinnamon
¼ teaspoon grated nutmeg

1½ tablespoons cornstarch
1 tablespoon butter
1 to 2 tablespoons Grand Marnier or other orange-flavored liqueur (optional)
Salt and freshly ground pepper

1. In a 3½-quart electric slow cooker, mix the carrots, orange juice concentrate, brown sugar, cinnamon, nutmeg, and 2 tablespoons water.

2. Cover and cook on the low heat setting about 7 hours, or until the carrots are almost tender. Increase the heat to the high setting.

3. Dissolve the cornstarch in 2 tablespoons cold water and stir into the carrots. Cook, covered, 30 minutes longer, or until slightly thickened. Stir in the butter and liqueur and season with salt and pepper to taste. Serve hot.

Creamed Corn

This enticing dish is a wonderful accompaniment to roast beef or any grilled meats. Once you start eating this, you can't stop—it's so good!

MAKES 8 SERVINGS

1 cup milk
1 cup heavy cream
2 tablespoons sugar
¾ teaspoon salt
2 teaspoons Worcestershire sauce
⅛ teaspoon cayenne

¼ cup quick-mixing flour, such as Wondra
3 (16-ounce) packages frozen whole kernel corn, thawed and drained
¼ cup grated Parmesan cheese
2 tablespoons chopped fresh parsley

1. In a 3½-quart electric slow cooker, whisk together the milk, cream, sugar, salt, Worcestershire sauce, cayenne, and flour until smooth. Stir in the corn.
2. Cover and cook on the high heat setting 3 to 3½ hours, stirring once or twice, until bubbly and thickened. Serve, garnished with the cheese and parsley.

Green Beans, Peppers, and Tomatoes with Balsamic Vinegar and Sun-Dried Tomatoes

This steamed vegetable potpourri is attractive and delicious whether served hot as a vegetable course or cold as a salad. It's also good topped with crumbled Gorgonzola, feta, or goat cheese. Be sure to use tender young green beans and cook until they are still a tad crisp, but still tender.

MAKES 6 SERVINGS

1 pound fresh green beans, cut into
   1½-inch-long pieces
3 tomatoes, halved and thinly sliced
1 onion, thinly sliced
1 large red bell pepper, halved and cut
   into thin strips
1 large green bell pepper, halved and
   cut into thin strips
3 garlic cloves, minced

1 (5¾-ounce) can pitted ripe olives,
   drained and coarsely chopped
3 tablespoons balsamic vinegar
3 tablespoons extra-virgin olive oil
1 teaspoon dried basil
½ teaspoon salt
½ teaspoon freshly ground pepper
⅓ cup slivered sun-dried tomato

1. In a 4-quart electric slow cooker, mix together the beans, tomatoes, onion, red and green bell peppers, garlic, olives, 2 tablespoons each of the vinegar and olive oil, the basil, salt, and pepper. Sprinkle the sun-dried tomatoes on top.

2. Cover and cook on the low heat setting about 3 hours, or just until the vegetables are crisp-tender. Stir to mix.

3. Drain off the excess cooking liquid and stir in the remaining 1 tablespoon each vinegar and olive oil. Serve warm, at room temperature, or chilled.

Potatoes with Fresh Fennel

Fennel looks like very fat celery, but has a subtle anise taste. Serve with meat, chicken, or fish.

MAKES 4 TO 6 SERVINGS

2 pounds baking potatoes, peeled, halved, and thinly sliced (about 5 medium potatoes)

1 red bell pepper, cut into thin strips

¾ cup homemade or canned vegetable or chicken broth

1 large fennel bulb (about 1½ pounds), quartered lengthwise and thinly sliced

Seasoned salt and garlic pepper

2 tablespoons extra-virgin oil (optional)

1. In a 3½-quart electric slow cooker, layer the potatoes and bell pepper strips. Pour on half of the broth. Top with all of the fennel pieces, covering the potatoes. Pour the remaining broth over all.

2. Cover and cook on the low heat setting 5 to 6 hours, or until the potatoes and fennel are tender. Season with seasoned salt and garlic pepper to taste; mix gently. For extra flavor, drizzle the oil on top.

Potatoes, Peppers, and Tomatoes

This is a wonderful combination and a good accompaniment to grilled chicken, fish, or beef. It also makes a good meatless main dish when topped with crumbled feta cheese.

MAKES 8 TO 10 SERVINGS

3 pounds red potatoes, scrubbed and cut into ¼-inch-thick slices or 1-inch cubes
1 teaspoon garlic pepper
3 tablespoons dried basil
1 onion, sliced
3 large tomatoes (about 1¼ pounds), thinly sliced

1 red bell pepper, cut into strips
1 green bell pepper, cut into strips
½ cup red wine vinegar
2 tablespoons olive oil
⅔ cup coarsely chopped pitted kalamata olives or 1 (5¾-ounce) can pitted ripe olives, drained and coarsely chopped

1. Arrange ⅓ of the potatoes in the bottom of a 6-quart electric slow cooker. Season with ⅓ of the garlic pepper and ½ tablespoon of the basil. Repeat in 2 more layers. Top with the onion, tomatoes, and bell pepper strips. Mix together the vinegar, olive oil, and remaining 1½ tablespoons basil. Pour evenly over all.
2. Cover and cook on the high heat setting 4½ to 5 hours, or until the potatoes are fork-tender but still hold their shape. Mix gently once or twice during cooking, if possible. Before serving, drain off the excess liquid, if desired. Stir in the olives. Serve hot or refrigerate and serve cold.

Red Cabbage and Apples

Cabbage shrinks considerably when cooked this way; so while it may seem like you're starting out with a lot, you really won't end up with as much as you think. This reminds me of my grandmother's cabbage and is one of my favorite ways to eat the vegetable. It's great hot from the slow cooker as well as chilled a day or two later.

MAKES 6 SERVINGS

1 large head of red cabbage, shredded (about 12 cups)

2 apples, seeded and chopped into small pieces

½ cup red wine vinegar

2 tablespoons water

3 tablespoons brown sugar

Seasoned salt

1. In a 5-quart electric slow cooker, combine the red cabbage and apples. Mix together the vinegar, water, and 2 tablespoons of the brown sugar. Pour over the cabbage mixture.

2. Cover and cook on the low heat setting 6 hours, or until the cabbage is tender. Stir in the remaining 1 tablespoon brown sugar and seasoned salt to taste. Serve immediately as a vegetable side dish or refrigerate until cold and serve chilled.

Rice with Porcini Mushrooms

Although dried porcini mushrooms are pricey, they're worth a splurge occasionally, because they impart rich, earthy flavor. Serve with grilled steak or chicken.

1½ cups converted white rice
3 cups homemade or canned vegetable
   or chicken broth
¾ cup dry white wine
1 ounce dried porcini mushrooms,
   rinsed quickly under hot running
   tap water to remove any grit

1 medium leek (white and tender
   green), well rinsed and chopped
3 tablespoons freshly grated imported
   Parmesan cheese

1. In a 3½-quart electric slow cooker, combine all the ingredients except the cheese. Stir to mix well.

2. Cover and cook on the low heat setting about 3 hours, or just until the rice is tender but not mushy. Stir in the Parmesan cheese and serve.

Vegetables Agro Dolce

This Italian sweet-and-sour medley makes a great appetizer or salad served on a colorful lettuce leaf.

1 large eggplant (1½ pounds), peeled and chopped
Salt
1 onion, thinly sliced into rounds, rings separated
1 medium red bell pepper, chopped
1 medium yellow bell pepper, chopped
1 medium green bell pepper, chopped
2 large celery ribs, chopped
2 medium zucchini, chopped
2 garlic cloves, crushed through a press

¼ cup red wine vinegar
3 tablespoons balsamic vinegar
2 tablespoons raisins
2 tablespoons drained capers
1 tablespoon extra-virgin olive oil
½ teaspoon garlic pepper
2 pinches of sugar
2 to 3 tablespoons pine nuts, toasted if desired

1. Spread the chopped eggplant out on a double thickness of paper towels. Sprinkle generously with salt. Let stand 1 hour.

2. Rinse the eggplant under cold water to remove the salt, drain well, and with your hands squeeze the eggplant to remove as much moisture as possible.

3. Meanwhile, in a 4- or 5-quart electric slow cooker, mix together the onion, bell peppers, celery, zucchini, garlic, and wine vinegar. Add the eggplant and stir to mix. Cover and cook on the low heat setting about 4½ hours, or until the vegetables are tender. Drain the vegetables into a colander and return to the slow cooker.

4. Add the balsamic vinegar, raisins, capers, olive oil, garlic pepper, ¼ teaspoon salt, and sugar. Increase the heat setting to high and cook, uncovered, stirring occasionally, 15 minutes. Stir in the pine nuts. Serve warm, at room temperature, or chilled.

Pineapple Cinnamon Squash

An easy and delicious way to fix banana squash. Be sure to remove enough of the rind so you cook only the tender flesh.

MAKES 6 SIDE-DISH SERVINGS

3 to 3¼ pounds banana or hubbard squash, rind removed and cut into 1- to 1½-inch cubes
1 (8-ounce) can unsweetened crushed pineapple

1 to 1½ teaspoons ground cinammon
⅓ cup packed brown sugar
1 tablespoon butter, cut into small pieces

1. Place the squash in a 3½- or 4-quart electric slow cooker. In a small bowl, mix together the pineapple with its liquid, cinnamon, brown sugar, and butter. Spoon over the squash and mix well.

2. Cover and cook on the low heat setting 6½ to 7 hours, or until the squash is tender. Stir gently to mix. Serve immediately.

Wild and White Rice with Cherries, Apricots, and Pecans

For best results, be sure to cook this rice dish on the low heat setting for the time specified. Also, you must use converted rice. Do not overcook, or you'll end up with mush. Serve with chicken, turkey, or ham.

MAKES ABOUT 8 TO 10 SERVINGS

1 cup converted white rice
1 cup wild rice, rinsed and drained
2 (14½-ounce) cans vegetable or
   chicken broth
½ cup hot water
¼ cup dry sherry
1 medium onion, chopped

¾ teaspoon garlic powder
½ teaspoon garlic pepper
½ cup chopped dried apricots
½ cup dried cherries
½ cup chopped pecans, toasted if
   desired
¼ cup chopped fresh parsley

1. In a 3½- or 4-quart electric slow cooker, mix together the white rice, wild rice, broth, water, sherry, onion, garlic powder, and garlic pepper.

2. Cover and cook on the low heat setting about 5 hours, or until the rices are tender but not mushy. Stir in the apricots, cherries, pecans, and parsley. Serve immediately.

Mexicali Rice

Next time you're serving south-of-the border fare, whip up a pot of this to offer alongside. Leftovers reheat well in the microwave oven the next day.

MAKES 12 SERVINGS

1 (15¼-ounce) can whole kernel corn, drained

1 (15-ounce) can black beans, rinsed and drained

1 (4-ounce) can diced green chiles

1 medium onion, chopped

1 red bell pepper, chopped

2 cups converted white rice

3½ cups boiling water

½ cup thawed frozen orange juice concentrate

6 tablespoons fresh lime juice (from about 3 limes)

1½ tablespoons ground cumin

1 tablespoon chili powder

⅓ cup chopped fresh cilantro

½ teaspoon salt

1. In a 4-quart electric slow cooker, mix together the corn, black beans, green chiles, onion, bell pepper, rice, boiling water, orange juice concentrate, ¼ cup of the lime juice, the cumin, and the chili powder.

2. Cover and cook on the low heat setting 2¾ to 3 hours. Stir in the remaining 2 tablespoons lime juice, the cilantro, and salt. Mix well. Serve hot.

Candied Yams

These yams are a yummy addition to holiday meals. Use yams with a vivid sweet orange flesh because they cook up to a much moister texture than pale sweet potatoes, which can end up dry and crumbly.

MAKES 8 TO 12 SERVINGS

3½ to 4 pounds yams, peeled and cut into 1-inch cubes
¾ cup packed dark brown sugar
4 tablespoons butter, melted
1½ teaspoons ground cinnamon
¼ teaspoon grated nutmeg

2 tablespoons fresh orange juice
3 tablespoons brandy (optional)
1½ teaspoons grated orange zest
1 cup miniature marshmallows
½ cup chopped toasted pecans

1. Place the yams in a 4-quart electric slow cooker. In a medium bowl, mix together the brown sugar, melted butter, cinnamon, nutmeg, and orange juice. Spoon over the yams.

2. Cover and cook on the low heat setting 5½ to 6 hours, stirring once, if possible, until the yams are tender.

3. Stir in the brandy and orange zest. Sprinkle the marshmallows and pecans over the top. Cover and cook 5 minutes longer, or until the marshmallows are melted. Serve immediately.

Lazy Apricot Preserves

Making jam doesn't get much simpler, and you don't need to worry about scorching or burning when a slow cooker is used. Since this recipe uses dried apricots, you can turn to it any time of year. Make an extra batch to give friends or relatives for a special gift.

MAKES ABOUT 4½ CUPS

1 pound dried apricots   3½ cups water
1¾ cups sugar

1. In a food processor, process the apricots until very finely chopped. Transfer to a 3½-quart electric slower cooker. Stir in the sugar and water.

2. Cover and cook on the high heat setting 2½ hours, stirring twice, if possible. Uncover and cook on high, stirring occasionally, 2 hours longer, or until the jam has thickened.

3. Ladle the jam into clean, hot canning or jam jars; seal according to the manufacturer's instructions with lids and ring bands. Process in a boiling water bath 10 to 15 minutes. Or let the jam cool and store in the refrigerator up to 3 weeks. For longer storage, freeze up to 3 months.

VARIATION:

APRICOT-ORANGE JAM: Stir in 1 tablespoon grated orange zest at the end of the cooking time.

Cranberry Orange Relish

You can make this easy relish up to a week in advance and refrigerate it. Or stash it in the freezer for up to 2 months. It's great as an accompaniment to turkey, chicken, or pork throughout the holiday season.

MAKES ABOUT 3 CUPS

1 (12-ounce) package fresh cranberries, rinsed and picked over

¼ cup thawed frozen orange juice concentrate

1 cup packed light brown sugar

2 tablespoons raspberry or cider vinegar

½ cup chopped dried apricots

½ cup golden raisins

½ cup chopped walnuts

1. In a 3½-quart electric slow cooker, mix together the cranberries, orange juice concentrate, brown sugar, and vinegar.

2. Cover and cook on the low heat setting about 3 hours, or until the cranberry skins pop. Turn off the heat.

3. Stir in the apricots, raisins, and walnuts. Cool, then transfer to a covered container and refrigerate.

Dried Fruit Chutney

This is a fabulous chutney you can make year-round. It makes a great hostess or holiday gift. To chop the dried fruits easily, use a pulse action in the food processor.

MAKES ABOUT 7½ CUPS

1 pound mixed dried fruits (apricots, peaches, apples, prunes), chopped

1 pound dried apricots, coarsely chopped

6 ounces pitted prunes (about 1 cup), coarsely chopped

½ cup raisins

1 medium onion, chopped

¾ cup sugar

2 cups water

1½ cups apple cider vinegar

2 teaspoons Madras curry powder

¼ teaspoon ground ginger

⅛ teaspoon cayenne

¼ teaspoon salt

1. In a 4- or 5-quart electric slow cooker, combine all the ingredients. Mix well.

2. Cover and cook on the low heat setting 4 to 5 hours, or until the fruits are tender but still retain their shape; do not overcook. Let cool, then refrigerate up to 3 weeks. For longer storage, freeze up to 3 months.

NOTE: To speed this up a bit, you can cook the chutney 1½ hours on the low heat setting and then 1½ hours on the high heat setting.

Pineapple Mango Chutney

The slow cooker lends itself to making wonderful chutneys, such as this one, which are much better tasting—and more economical—than many of the commercial varieties. This makes a great accompaniment to roast pork, chicken, or beef and to all kinds of curries.

MAKES ABOUT 5 CUPS

1 (20-ounce) can unsweetened crushed pineapple, liquid reserved
1 semiripe mango, peeled, pitted, and cut into ¾-inch pieces
¾ cup packed brown sugar
½ cup red wine vinegar
¼ cup fresh lime juice
¼ teaspoon garlic powder
¼ teaspoon ground ginger
1 medium onion, chopped
1 cup shredded or flaked coconut
1 cup raisins
1 (3-inch) cinnamon stick
1 to 2 tablespoons chopped fresh green chiles

1. In a 3½-quart electric slow cooker, mix together all the ingredients.
2. Cover and cook on the low heat setting 6 to 6½ hours.
3. Remove the lid and increase the heat to the high setting. Cook, uncovered, 2 hours longer, or until the mixture is slightly thickened. Remove the cinnamon stick. Let cool to room temperature, then refrigerate and use within 2 weeks or freeze up to 2 months.

Hot Curried Fruit

Tangy fruits make an excellent accompaniment to ham or turkey as well as an interesting condiment for brunch with quiche or simple egg dishes.

MAKES 8 TO 10 SERVINGS

2 (20-ounce) cans unsweetened pineapple chunks
1 (29-ounce) can fruit cocktail
1 (29-ounce) can sliced cling peaches
1 (17-ounce) can apricot halves

2 tablespoons butter
½ cup packed brown sugar
2½ teaspoons Madras curry powder
1 tablespoon cornstarch
1 tablespoon cold water

1. Drain all the fruits well. Turn into a 3½-quart electric slow cooker. In a small glass bowl or measure, heat the butter in a microwave oven on high power 30 to 40 seconds, or until melted. Stir in the brown sugar and curry powder until well blended. Pour over the fruits; stir gently.
2. Cover and cook on the high heat setting 2½ hours.
3. Dissolve the cornstarch in the cold water and stir into the fruit mixture. Cook, uncovered, on high heat 30 minutes longer, or until thickened slightly.

Chapter Eight
Desserts and Beverages

When people find out that a dessert came from the slow cooker, they're always amazed. They don't give a second thought to preparing chilis, stews, or beans in a slow cooker, but dessert—hard to believe! Many slow-cooker buffs never explored the possibilities, which are numerous.

Granted, there are limits and not every dessert is a candidate for slow cooking (no pies, cookies, standard layer cakes, etc.), but then not every appliance is well suited to making everything under the sun. Some desserts are better baked in an oven, prepared in the microwave, or on top of the stove.

But the slow cooker turns out wonderful cozy bread puddings, steamed puddings, crème brûlées and other custards, pudding cakes, fruit desserts, moist dense fruitcakes, and even cheesecakes. Although some manufacturers offer a special bread and cake baking pan, I opted to stick with standard equipment that is readily available to most cooks. For a sampling of what's feasible and just how easily you can turn out a homey, comforting creation, peruse the desserts in the pages that follow.

Before you get started making desserts, here are some handy hints:

Check your dishes and equipment before making a slow-cooker dessert. If a dish or pan is required for a specific dessert, make sure it will fit into the slow cooker you'll be using, with a little space between the sides of the cooker and the dish.

Cheesecakes in the recipes here require a 5-quart slow cooker, an 8-inch springform pan, and a collapsible vegetable steamer (or other low stable rack) to serve as a level baking rack or trivet in the bottom of the slow cooker. Make sure everything fits together before you begin recipe preparations.

Some of the other desserts require a 5-quart slow cooker, a 2½-quart soufflé dish, and a rack. Once again, give the equipment a trial run to see how the parts work together before you start making a recipe. Depending on the consistency of the mixture to be added to the soufflé dish, sometimes it's easier to add it after the dish is already positioned in the slow cooker.

Many of the desserts require a water bath around the dish in the slow cooker. When adding water, do so carefully so none of it splashes into the dessert batter. Or pour the water in first and then carefully set the dish holding the dessert preparation into the cooker.

Keep in mind that desserts must be cooked at the heat settings listed in individual recipes. Unlike with stews, meats, and chilis, if you switch from high to low heat settings or vice versa, the dessert may not rise or cook quickly enough to set, which could be a disaster. As you'll notice, desserts cook much more quickly than other dishes in a slow cooker, so plan accordingly.

Hot beverages are always popular when the wind is howling outside, on blustery days, in the snowy mountains, or during the holidays to warm the spirits. The slow cooker is terrific for preparing hot brews without fuss and keeping them warm while you're serving a crowd.

Dried Fruit and Zucchini Cake

This unusual cake, filled with dried apricots, raisins, and walnuts, bakes into a 3½-inch-tall round. Just before giving or serving, you can glaze the top with apricot preserves.

1 stick (4 ounces) butter, melted
2 eggs
1½ cups packed brown sugar
1 tablespoon vanilla extract
4 teaspoons ground cinnamon
1 teaspoon grated nutmeg
2 cups all-purpose flour
1½ teaspoons baking soda

¼ teaspoon baking powder
¼ teaspoon salt
1½ cups packed shredded zucchini
1½ cups coarsely chopped walnuts
1½ cups chopped dried apricots
1 cup raisins
¼ cup brandy

1. In a large bowl, beat together the butter, eggs, brown sugar, vanilla, cinnamon, and nutmeg until well blended. Stir in the flour, baking soda, baking powder, and salt until mixed. Add the zucchini, walnuts, apricots, and raisins and blend well. Scrape the batter into a buttered 3½-quart electric slow cooker.

2. Cover and cook on the high heat setting 2½ to 3 hours, or until a cake tester inserted in the center comes out clean. Remove the lid. Carefully, using potholders or mitts, remove the ceramic liner from the slow cooker and place on a rack.

3. Sprinkle the brandy over the top and around the edges of the warm cake. Let stand until almost cool. To unmold, run a sharp knife around the inside edges of the cooker and with a large spatula, lift out the cake in one piece. Let cool completely. To store, wrap the cake well in plastic wrap and then in foil. Refrigerate up to 1 week or freeze up to 3 months.

Candy Bar Cheesecake

You'll be amazed at how adeptly a slow cooker "bakes" a cheesecake. This one is particularly attractive because of the dark chocolate ganache topping.

MAKES 8 TO 10 SERVINGS

Chocolate Cookie Crust (recipe follows)
2 (8-ounce) packages cream cheese, softened
⅔ cup sugar
2 eggs
1 teaspoon vanilla extract
¼ cup plus 2 tablespoons heavy cream

1 tablespoon all-purpose flour
2 peanut butter or regular Snickers bars (2 ounces each), chopped
¾ cup semisweet chocolate chips
1 tablespoon light corn syrup
⅓ cup chopped walnuts, peanuts, or pecans

1. Prepare the Chocolate Cookie Crust. Set aside.

2. In a medium bowl, beat together the cream cheese, sugar, eggs, and vanilla with an electric mixer on high speed until smooth. Add ¼ cup heavy cream and the flour and beat on medium speed 1 to 2 minutes, or until fluffy. Turn half of the cream cheese mixture into the Chocolate Cookie Crust. Evenly sprinkle on the chopped candy. Top with the remaining cream cheese mixture, spreading evenly. Carefully cover the top of the pan with foil.

3. Place the cheesecake on a vegetable steamer or other rack set in the bottom of a 5-quart electric slow cooker. Cover and cook on the high heat setting 2¾ to 3 hours, or until the cheesecake is set. (Do not attempt to cook on the low heat setting for a longer time.) Remove the lid from the cooker and turn the cooker off. Let the cheesecake stand in the cooker until cool enough to handle. Remove and cool to room temperature, then refrigerate several hours or overnight, until cold.

4. When the cheesecake is cold, make the chocolate ganache topping. In a 1-cup glass measure, combine the chocolate chips, remaining 2 tablespoons cream, and corn syrup. Heat in a microwave oven on high power 1 minute, or until the chocolate is melted and smooth when stirred. Cool slightly. Spread the chocolate ganache evenly over the top of the cold cheesecake. Sprinkle on the chopped nuts. Return to the refrigerator and chill until the chocolate is set. To serve, remove the springform side from the pan and cut the cheesecake into slices. Refrigerate any leftovers.

CHOCOLATE COOKIE CRUST: In a medium bowl, mix together 1 cup chocolate cookie wafer crumbs, 1 tablespoon sugar, and 3 tablespoons melted butter until well blended. Press into the bottom and ¾ inch up the side of an 8-inch springform pan.

Lemon Cheesecake

You'll need a 5-quart round slow cooker and an 8-inch springform pan that fits inside it to make this cheesecake. This springform is set on top of a steamer or rack to allow for even cooking and heat circulation around the pan, but no water is necessary in the pot.

Graham Cracker Crumb Crust (recipe follows)

2 (8-ounce) packages cream cheese, softened

¾ cup sugar

2 eggs

1 teaspoon lemon extract

⅓ cup heavy cream

1 tablespoon all-purpose flour

½ cup prepared lemon curd

1. Prepare the Graham Cracker Crumb Crust. Set aside.

2. In a medium bowl, beat together the cream cheese and sugar with an electric mixer on high speed until smooth and creamy. Add the eggs, lemon extract, cream, and flour and beat on medium speed 2 to 3 minutes, or until smooth and fluffy. Spoon half of the cream cheese mixture into the graham cracker crust. Using half of the lemon curd, drop small spoonfuls over the top of the cheese mixture. Carefully top with the remaining cream cheese mixture. Drop small spoonfuls of the remaining lemon curd on top. With a knife, swirl the lemon curd slightly through the cheese mixture.

3. Place the cheesecake on a vegetable steamer or other low rack set in the bottom of a 5-quart electric slow cooker. Cover and cook on the high heat setting 2½ to 2¾ hours, or until set. (Do not attempt to cook on the low heat setting for a longer time.) Remove the lid from the cooker and turn the cooker off. Let the cheesecake stand in the cooker until cool enough to handle. Remove and cool to room temperature, then refrigerate several hours or overnight, until cold. To serve, remove the side from the springform pan and cut the cheesecake into slices. Garnish with additional whipped cream, if desired. Refrigerate any leftovers.

GRAHAM CRACKER CRUMB CRUST: In a medium bowl, mix together 1 cup graham cracker crumbs, 1 tablespoon sugar, and 3 tablespoons melted butter until well blended. Press into the bottom and ¾ inch up the side of an 8-inch springform pan.

Mascarpone Cheesecake with Blackberry Sauce

This creation was inspired by one I sampled at Stars Cafe in San Francisco a few years back. Mascarpone, a soft Italian fresh cheese, is now available in the cheese section of many supermarkets.

MAKES 8 TO 10 SERVINGS

1 cup finely ground amaretti cookies or coconut macaroon cookies (or ½ cup graham cracker crumbs mixed with ½ cup flaked coconut)

3 tablespoons butter, melted

2 (8-ounce) packages cream cheese, softened

½ pound mascarpone cheese

¾ cup granulated sugar

2 eggs

1 teaspoon vanilla extract

1 (16-ounce) package frozen unsweetened blackberries or raspberries, thawed

½ cup powdered sugar

1. In a medium bowl, mix together the cookie crumbs and melted butter until well mixed. Press into the bottom and ½ inch up the side of an 8-inch springform pan.
2. In a food processor, combine the cream cheese, mascarpone, granulated sugar, eggs, and vanilla. Process until smooth and creamy. Scrape the cheese filling into the crust.
3. Place a vegetable steamer or other low rack on the bottom of a 5-quart electric cooker. Pour 1 cup hot water into cooker. Set the cheesecake on the rack.
4. Cover and cook on the high setting about 3 hours, or until set. (Do not attempt to cook on the low heat setting for a longer time.) Remove the lid from the cooker and turn off the cooker. Allow the cheesecake to stand in the cooker until cool

186   Desserts and Beverages

enough to handle. Remove and cool to room temperature, then refrigerate several hours or overnight, until cold.

5. To make the blackberry sauce, puree the thawed berries in a food processor until smooth. Add the powdered sugar and blend well. To remove the seeds, press through a wire strainer into a bowl, pressing on the pulp and scraping the mixture from the underside of the strainer into the bowl. Refrigerate until serving time.

6. To serve, remove the springform side from the pan and cut the cheesecake into slices. Serve on dessert plates and top each slice with about 2½ tablespoons blackberry sauce. Refrigerate any leftovers.

Chocolate Applesauce Cake

When you don't want to heat up the oven, make this cake in your slow cooker. Be sure to use the high heat setting and to check the cake as it nears the end of its cooking time so you don't overbake it.

MAKES 8 TO 10 SERVINGS

6 tablespoons butter
1 cup granulated sugar
1 cup unsweetened applesauce
1 teaspoon ground cinnamon
1 teaspoon vanilla extract
3 eggs
4 (1-ounce) squares unsweetened chocolate, melted

1½ cups all-purpose flour
2 teaspoons baking soda
1 teaspoon baking powder
Pinch of salt
⅓ cup buttermilk
¾ cup semisweet chocolate chips
½ cup chopped walnuts
Sifted powdered sugar

1. In a large bowl, beat together the butter and granulated sugar with an electric mixer on high speed 1 to 2 minutes, or until fluffy. Beat in the applesauce, cinnamon, vanilla, and eggs until well mixed. Beat in the melted chocolate until blended. Add the flour, baking soda, baking powder, and salt. With the mixer on low speed, beat in the dry ingredients, adding the buttermilk as you beat. Beat just until evenly mixed. By hand, stir in the chocolate chips and walnuts. Scrape the batter into a buttered 3½-quart electric slow cooker and smooth the top.
2. Cover and cook on the high heat setting 2¼ to 2½ hours, or until a cake tester inserted in the center comes out clean. (Do not cook on the low heat setting for a longer time.)

3. Remove the lid and let the cake stand in the slow cooker until just barely warm. To unmold, run a sharp knife around the inside edges of the cooker and with a large spatula, carefully lift out the cake in one piece. Sprinkle powdered sugar over the top and cut into wedges to serve.

Holiday Steamed Fruitcake

Here is an easy, slow-cooker version of traditional fruitcake. It is moist and flavorful, served warm with a tangy citrus glaze. If you want to store it, sprinkle with a few tablespoons of brandy or orange liqueur and freeze, tightly wrapped.

MAKES 10 TO 12 SERVINGS

1 (18½-ounce) package pudding-in-cluded yellow cake mix
3 eggs
1 stick (4 ounces) butter, melted
1¼ cups milk
1 teaspoon ground cardamom
1 teaspoon ground cinnamon
1 teaspoon ground coriander
½ teaspoon ground allspice
½ teaspoon ground ginger
½ teaspoon ground mace
½ teaspoon grated nutmeg
¼ cup dried cranberries
¼ cup dark raisins
¼ cup golden raisins
2 tablespoons candied lemon peel
2 tablespoons candied orange peel
2 tablespoons candied citron
½ cup chopped pecans
1 tablespoon sugar
Citrus Glaze (recipe follows)

1. Place a vegetable steamer or other low rack in the bottom of a 5-quart electric slow cooker. Pour in 4 cups hot tap water and turn on the low heat setting.
2. In the large bowl of an electric mixer, combine the cake mix, eggs, melted butter, milk, cardamom, cinnamon, coriander, allspice, ginger, mace, and nutmeg. Beat on low speed 20 to 30 seconds to combine the ingredients, then beat on medium speed 2 minutes. Fold in the dried cranberries, dark and golden raisins, candied lemon and orange peels, citron, and pecans.

3. Sprinkle a 2½-quart soufflé dish that fits in the 5-quart slow cooker with the sugar. Turn the cake batter into the soufflé dish, spreading the top even. Place a buttered round of waxed paper on the top and then wrap the dish completely in a double thickness of aluminum foil. Tie with kitchen string to resemble a package for ease in lowering into the pot and removing. Place on the rack in the slow cooker. **4.** Cover and cook on the low heat setting 6 hours. Turn off the heat and let cool, covered, in the slow cooker 2 hours. To serve, cut into wedges and drizzle glaze on top. Serve warm or at room temperature.

CITRUS GLAZE: In a small nonreactive saucepan, mix together 2 teaspoons cornstarch, 1 cup orange marmalade, and 2 tablespoons lemon juice. Cook over medium heat, stirring constantly, until thickened, about 5 to 6 minutes.

Old-Fashioned Pumpkin Cake

Be sure that the 2½-quart soufflé dish you plan to use will fit into your 5-quart slow cooker before proceeding. To dress up this moist cake, reminiscent of a steamed pudding, top slices with whipped cream flavored with a little orange zest or Grand Marnier. Or sprinkle the top of the cake with powdered sugar before slicing.

MAKES 12 SERVINGS

½ cup vegetable oil
2 eggs
1½ cups sugar
1 cup canned solid-pack pumpkin
½ cup water
1½ cups all-purpose flour
1 teaspoon baking soda

¼ teaspoon baking powder
½ teaspoon ground cinnamon
½ teaspoon ground cloves
½ teaspoon grated nutmeg
⅛ teaspoon salt
¾ cup chopped pecans

1. In a large bowl, mix together the oil, eggs, sugar, pumpkin, and water. Add the flour, baking soda, baking powder, cinnamon, cloves, nutmeg, and salt. Blend well. Stir in the pecans. Turn into a buttered 2½-quart round soufflé dish. Carefully place the soufflé dish in a 5-quart electric slow cooker.

2. Cover and cook on the high heat setting about 3½ to 3¾ hours, or until a cake tester inserted in center of the cake comes out clean. (Do not attempt to cook on the low heat setting for a longer time.)

3. Remove the lid and turn the cooker off. Leave the cake in the cooker until the dish is cool enough to handle. Remove from the cooker. Cut into wedges and serve warm or at room temperature.

Double Chocolate-Orange Pudding Cake

Filled with old-fashioned goodness, this dessert works well in a slow cooker. Orange zest and chocolate chips give it extra pizzazz.

MAKES 4 TO 6 SERVINGS

1 cup all-purpose flour
¾ cup granulated sugar
¼ cup plus 3 tablespoons unsweetened cocoa powder
2 teaspoons baking powder
¼ teaspoon salt
½ cup milk

3 tablespoons butter, melted
1 tablespoon grated orange zest
½ cup semisweet chocolate chips
¾ cup packed light brown sugar
1⅔ cups hot water
Whipped cream or chocolate ice cream

1. In a medium bowl, mix together the flour, granulated sugar, 3 tablespoons of the cocoa, the baking powder, and the salt until well blended. Stir in the milk, butter, orange zest, and chocolate chips and mix well. Turn the batter into a 3½-quart electric slow cooker.

2. In another bowl, mix together the brown sugar and remaining ¼ cup cocoa until well blended. Sprinkle over the batter. Gently pour the water evenly over all; *do not stir.*

3. Cover and cook on the high heat setting about 1¾ to 2 hours, or until a tester inserted in the cake portion of the dessert comes out clean. (Do not cook on the low heat setting for a longer time.) Serve warm or at room temperature, topped with whipped cream.

Chocolate Raspberry Strata

This dessert strata is a kind of bread pudding. Designed to be cooked on the high heat setting, it's ready to enjoy in two hours.

MAKES ABOUT 6 SERVINGS

6 cups (1-inch) cubes Hawaiian bread, Challah, or brioche
1½ cups semisweet chocolate chips
½ pint container (about 6 ounces) fresh raspberries (do not substitute frozen), rinsed and drained

½ cup heavy cream
½ cup milk
4 eggs
¼ cup sugar
1 teaspoon vanilla extract
Whipped cream

1. Place half of the bread cubes in a well-buttered 3½-quart electric slow cooker. Sprinkle on half of the chocolate chips and raspberries. Cover with the remaining bread cubes, then top with the remaining chocolate chips and raspberries.

2. In a medium bowl, whisk together the cream, milk, eggs, sugar, and vanilla until well blended. Pour evenly over the bread mixture in the cooker.

3. Cover and cook on the high heat setting about 1¾ to 2 hours, or until set. (Do not cook on the low heat setting for a longer time.) Let stand 5 to 10 minutes before serving. Serve garnished with whipped cream.

Chocolate Bread Pudding

My kids, who love chocolate, gave this a thumbs-up rating, and they couldn't get enough! Serve warm, topped with whipped cream or vanilla ice cream.

MAKES 5 TO 6 SERVINGS

2½ cups milk

4 (1-ounce) squares unsweetened chocolate, cut into small pieces

3 eggs

1 cup sugar

2 teaspoons vanilla extract

4 cups loosely packed ¾-inch cubes stale sourdough or country French bread

Whipped cream

1. In a large glass bowl, combine the milk and chocolate. Heat in a microwave oven on high power about 6 minutes, stirring every 2 minutes, until the chocolate is melted and the mixture is smooth. (Or heat in a large saucepan over medium heat, stirring often.) Whisk in the eggs, sugar, and vanilla, blending until smooth. Stir in the bread cubes.

2. Place a 2½-quart soufflé dish in the bottom of a 5-quart electric slow cooker. Add 1 to 1½ cups hot water to the cooker around the outside of the dish so that it reaches halfway up the sides of the dish. Carefully pour the chocolate-bread mixture into the soufflé dish.

3. Cover and cook on the high heat setting 2½ hours. (Do not cook on the low heat setting for a longer time.) Remove the lid from the cooker and cook on high 20 to 30 minutes longer, or until set. Let the pudding stand in the slow cooker until the dish is cool enough to remove. Serve the pudding warm, topped with whipped cream. Refrigerate any leftovers.

Pumpkin Bread Pudding

3 eggs
1 (16-ounce) can solid-pack pumpkin
1½ teaspoons ground cinnamon
½ teaspoon grated nutmeg
¼ teaspoon ground cloves
3 tablespoons sweet sherry

¾ cup sugar
2 cups milk
3 cups packed ¾-inch cubes Italian, French, or sourdough bread
½ cup chopped walnuts
Heavy cream

1. In a large bowl, whisk the eggs until smooth. Whisk in the pumpkin, cinnamon, nutmeg, and cloves until well mixed. Whisk in the sherry, sugar, and milk until smooth. Stir in the bread cubes and nuts. Turn the mixture into a 3½-quart electric slow cooker.

2. Cover and cook on the high heat setting 2¼ to 2½ hours, or until puffed. (Do not cook on the low heat setting for a longer time.) Remove the lid and continue cooking on high 20 to 30 minutes longer. Serve warm or at room temperature, topped with heavy cream.

Turtle Pudding

This dessert is a divine combination of chocolate, nuts, and caramel. Served with a dollop of whipped cream or a scoop of ice cream, it is the perfect way to end a meal.

MAKES 6 TO 8 SERVINGS

1 (21½-ounce) package brownie mix
½ cup water
¼ cup vegetable oil
1 egg

1 cup semisweet chocolate chips
1 cup chopped walnuts or pecans
13 caramel candies, unwrapped
Whipped cream or vanilla ice cream

1. Place a vegetable steamer or other low rack on the bottom of a 5-quart electric slow cooker. Pour in 4 cups hot tap water and turn on the high heat setting.

2. In a large bowl, combine the brownie mix, water, oil, and egg. Beat to mix well. Stir in the chocolate chips and nuts.

3. Butter and dust with sugar a 2½-quart soufflé dish that fits in the 5-quart slow cooker. Turn the brownie mixture into the dish. Push the caramels partially into the top, but do not cover completely with the brownie mixture. Wrap the dish in a double thickness of foil. Tie with kitchen string to resemble a package for ease in lowering into the pot and removing. Place on the rack in the slow cooker.

4. Cover and cook on the high heat setting 4½ hours. Remove the dish from the slow cooker, uncover, and let cool 30 minutes. Serve warm, with whipped cream or ice cream.

Berry-Peach Cobbler

This dessert is downright homey and delicious. Don't expect the cobbler topping to be browned—but do expect it to taste good.

MAKES 6 TO 8 SERVINGS

1 (16-ounce) package frozen unsweetened blackberries, thawed but not drained

1 (16-ounce) package frozen mixed unsweetened berries (raspberries, blueberries, and strawberries) OR 1 (16-ounce) package frozen unsweetened raspberries, thawed but not drained

1 (16-ounce) package frozen unsweetened peach slices, thawed but not drained

¾ cup granulated sugar

1⅓ cups all-purpose flour

3 tablespoons brown sugar

1¼ teaspoons baking powder

¼ teaspoon grated nutmeg

¼ teaspoon salt

6 tablespoons butter, cut up

½ cup heavy cream

1 teaspoon vanilla extract

1½ teaspoons cinnamon-sugar

Sweetened whipped cream

1. In a 4-quart electric slow cooker, combine the fruits with their juices, granulated sugar, and ⅓ cup flour. Mix well.

2. Cover and cook on the high heat setting 1 to 1¼ hours. Stir well.

3. Just before the time is up, in a food processor fitted with a metal blade, combine the remaining 1 cup flour, brown sugar, baking powder, nutmeg, and salt. Process to mix well. Add the butter and process until cut into fine crumbs. Add the cream and vanilla and process until the mixture holds together and forms a soft ball. Drop spoonfuls of the dough evenly on top of the fruit. Dust the mounds of dough lightly with the cinnamon-sugar.

4. Cover and continue cooking on high (do not cook on the low heat setting as the dough will not cook properly) about 1½ hours, or until the dough is cooked through. Serve with whipped cream.

Custard with Fruit

This is a silky smooth crème brûlée–style custard without the caramelized sugar topping. Serve topped with fresh berries or for a special treat, spoon the custard over cake slices.

MAKES 5 TO 6 SERVINGS

5 cold egg yolks
⅓ cup sugar
1¼ cups heavy cream
1 teaspoon vanilla extract

1 pint basket raspberries, rinsed and drained, or strawberries, rinsed and sliced

1. Place a vegetable steamer or other low rack in a 3½- or 4-quart electric slow cooker that will hold a 1-quart soufflé dish. Add 2½ to 3 cups warm tap water to the cooker.

2. In a medium bowl, whisk together the egg yolks and sugar until well blended. Whisk in the cream and vanilla until well mixed. Turn the mixture into a buttered 1-quart soufflé dish. Cover with foil. Make two handles by folding two 20- to 22-inch-long pieces of foil lengthwise into quarters and placing them crisscross underneath and up around the soufflé dish to use for lifting it in and out of the pot. Place the soufflé dish on the rack in the slow cooker.

3. Cover and cook on the high heat setting about 1¾ to 2 hours, or until the pudding is set and a knife inserted in the center comes out clean. Using the foil handles, carefully lift the dish out of the cooker. Cool to room temperature, then cover with plastic wrap and refrigerate until well chilled. Serve the custard topped with berries.

Cinnamon Applesauce

The slow cooker is the ideal way to cook applesauce effortlessly. Vary the apple variety according to the season's best buys. For a special treat, serve the warm applesauce over vanilla ice cream and drizzle a little jarred caramel sauce on top.

MAKES ABOUT 3½ CUPS

3½ pounds Granny Smith apples, peeled, cored, and sliced
½ cup packed brown sugar

1½ tablespoons fresh lemon juice
¼ teaspoon ground cinnamon

1. In a 3½-quart electric slow cooker, toss together the apples, brown sugar, and lemon juice.

2. Cover and cook on the high heat setting 3 hours, or until the apples are very tender. Mash up the apples with a potato masher. Stir in the cinnamon. Serve warm, at room temperature, or cold.

Spiced Apples with Dried Cherries and Apricots

This warm, homestyle dessert is a nice ending to any meal. If you have two slow cookers, you can make the main dish in one and the dessert in the other.

MAKES 6 TO 8 SERVINGS

2½ pounds Granny Smith apples, peeled, cored, and cut into 8 wedges each

⅔ cup dried cherries

1 (6-ounce) package dried apricots, chopped

1 teaspoon grated lemon zest

2 tablespoons fresh lemon juice

1 cup packed brown sugar

1½ teaspoons ground cinnamon

1 teaspoon grated nutmeg

½ teaspoon ground coriander

¼ cup all-purpose flour

½ teaspoon salt

4 tablespoons butter, cut into small pieces

Crunchy Topping (recipe follows)

Ice cream, whipped cream, or Cheddar cheese slices

1. In a large bowl, combine the apples, dried fruits, lemon zest, lemon juice, brown sugar, cinnamon, nutmeg, coriander, flour, salt, and butter. Toss until well mixed. Turn into a 3½- or 4-quart electric slow cooker.

2. Cover and cook on the low heat setting about 6 hours, or until the apples are soft but still hold their shape.

3. Meanwhile, make the Crunchy Topping and set aside to cool. Sprinkle half of the Crunchy Topping over the fruit and cook, covered, on low 30 minutes longer. Serve with ice cream, whipped cream, or cheese. Pass the remaining Crunchy Topping separately.

CRUNCHY TOPPING: In a medium saucepan, melt 4 tablespoons butter. Add 1 cup old-fashioned rolled oats and 1 cup chopped pecans. Cook over medium heat, stirring occasionally, 5 minutes. Add ¾ cup packed brown sugar, 1½ teaspoons ground cinnamon, 1 teaspoon grated nutmeg, and ½ teaspoon ground coriander. Cook 5 minutes longer.

Chocolate Fondue or Fudge Sauce

This versatile mixture can double as a fondue dipping sauce for assorted fresh fruits, marshmallows, or cake pieces and as a fudge sauce to top ice creams, sorbets, fresh fruits, or cake slices.

MAKES ABOUT 1¾ CUPS

12 ounces semisweet chocolate chips or semisweet chocolate, broken into small pieces
1 (1-ounce) square unsweetened chocolate, cut up.

⅔ cup heavy cream or half-and-half
1 teaspoon vanilla extract
Cut-up fresh fruits, large marshmallows, cubes of cake, ice cream, or sorbet

1. In a 1-quart mini electric slow cooker, combine the chocolates and cream.
2. Cover, plug in, and cook 1¼ hours, stirring twice, until the mixture is melted, smooth, and hot. Stir in the vanilla. Serve hot or warm with fresh fruits, marshmallows, and cake cubes for dipping or serve over ice cream, sorbet, fruits, and/or cake. Refrigerate any leftover sauce.

VARIATIONS:

CHOCOLATE-ORANGE FONDUE OR SAUCE: Stir in 1 tablespoon grated orange zest along with the vanilla.

ESPRESSO FONDUE OR SAUCE: Stir in 1 tablespoon instant espresso powder with the vanilla.

CHEWY FUDGE SAUCE: For a chewier fudge sauce for ice cream, stir in 1 to 2 tablespoons light corn syrup with the vanilla.

NOTE: The recipe above can be doubled and cooked in a 3½-quart electric slow cooker. Cover and cook on the low heat setting 2¾ to 3 hours, stirring once or twice, until the chocolate melts and the mixture is smooth and hot. Makes about 3¾ cups. Refrigerate any leftovers in convenient-size containers, as the chocolate mixture hardens into one large mass and is difficult to break up into small amounts.

Hot Mulled Cider

This aromatic drink flavored with cinnamon and cloves is great served hot from the slow cooker, especially during the holidays or the chilly winter months. Refrigerate any leftovers and reheat or serve chilled.

MAKES ABOUT 20 (½-CUP) SERVINGS

2 quarts unsweetened apple cider
1 cup pineapple juice
1 (12-ounce) can frozen orange juice concentrate, thawed
¼ cup packed brown sugar

3 cinnamon sticks
6 whole cloves
Thin orange or lemon slices, for garnish

1. In a 3½- or 4-quart electric slow cooker, combine the apple cider, pineapple juice, undiluted orange juice concentrate, brown sugar, cinnamon sticks, and cloves. Mix well.

2. Cover and cook on the low heat setting 5 to 6 hours. Remove and discard the cinnamon sticks and cloves. Serve hot in mugs or heatproof punch cups, garnished with orange or lemon slices. Refrigerate any leftovers and reheat in a microwave oven or serve chilled.

Warm Spirited Mocha

Put on a pot of this dessert coffee just before guests arrive for dinner, and it'll be ready in time for dessert.

MAKES 10 SERVINGS

8 cups brewed cold coffee, chocolate flavored if desired

¾ cup sweet ground chocolate and cocoa mix (such as Ghirardelli)

½ cup Grand Marnier or other orange liqueur

½ cup Kahlúa or other coffee liqueur

1 cup heavy cream, whipped

1. In a 3½-quart electric slow cooker, combine the coffee and ground chocolate mix. Stir to blend well.

2. Cover and cook on the high heat setting 2 to 2½ hours, or until very hot.

3. Stir in the Grand Marnier and Kahlúa. Ladle into mugs or heatproof stemmed glasses. Top with a spoonful or two of whipped cream and serve. The coffee can be kept warm on the low heat setting for 1 hour.

No-Alcohol Party Punch

This fruity blend appeals to children and adults alike. It's a simple recipe to turn to anytime you want a heartwarming punch to serve on a cold day or blustery night.

MAKES ABOUT 12 (¾-CUP) SERVINGS

1 (12-ounce) can frozen orange juice concentrate, thawed
1 (12-ounce) can frozen raspberry juice blend concentrate, thawed

7 cups water
½ large lemon, sliced
1 cinnamon stick
2 to 3 oranges, thinly sliced

1. In a 3½-quart electric slow cooker, mix together the orange juice concentrate, raspberry juice blend concentrate, water, lemon slices, and cinnamon stick.

2. Cover and cook on the low heat setting 4 to 5 hours, or until hot. Strain and discard the lemon slices and cinnamon stick. Return the punch to the slow cooker to keep warm.

3. To serve, ladle into heatproof punch cups. Float an orange slice on the top of each serving. The slow cooker will keep the punch at serving temperature 1 to 2 hours.

Hot Tropical Spiced Tea

Tea makes a wonderful basis for fruit punches. Garnish with a slice of orange or a sprig of fresh mint.

MAKES 8 TO 10 SERVINGS

⅓ cup sugar/no-lemon iced tea mix
6 cups water
1 (12-ounce) can frozen tropical fruit
   juice blend concentrate, thawed

½ orange, thinly sliced
2 (3-inch) cinnamon sticks
1½ to 2 tablespoons sugar

1. In a 3½-quart electric slow cooker, mix together the dry tea mix, tropical juice concentrate, orange slices, and cinnamon sticks.

2. Cover and cook on the low heat setting 4 to 5 hours, or until very hot. Strain and discard the orange slices and cinnamon sticks. Return the tea mixture to the slow cooker. Add sugar as needed. The punch can be kept hot in the slow cooker 1 to 2 hours while serving.

Holiday Wassail

Although this isn't a traditional wassail because it doesn't contain ale or wine, it's a terrific recipe that we've referred to by that name for years. A colleague gave me this recipe, and it's a spiced drink I've served at holiday parties over the years with great success. Using the slow cooker makes it hassle-free and easy on the hostess as no tending is required. You can spike it with rum or brandy, if you wish.

MAKES ABOUT 24 (½-CUP) SERVINGS

6 cups apple juice

1 (32-ounce) container cranberry-raspberry juice cocktail or cranberry juice cocktail

1 (6-ounce) can frozen orange juice concentrate, thawed

1 (6-ounce) can frozen lemonade concentrate, thawed

1 cup packed brown sugar

2 cups water

4 (2½- to 3-inch) cinnamon sticks

1 orange, cut into 4 horizontal slices

1 teaspoon whole cloves

1 tablespoon Angostura bitters

2 cups rum (optional)

1. In a 6-quart electric slow cooker, combine the apple juice, cranberry raspberry juice, undiluted orange juice concentrate, undiluted lemonade, sugar, water, cinnamon sticks, orange slices studded with the cloves, and bitters.

2. Cover and cook on the low heat setting 6 to 7 hours. Just before serving, stir in the rum, if desired. Remove and discard the cinnamon sticks and orange slices with cloves. Serve hot in mugs or heatproof punch cups. Refrigerate any leftovers and reheat in a microwave oven or serve chilled.

Index